So What Makes Our Teaching Christian?

So What Makes Our Teaching Christian?

Teaching in the Name, Spirit, and Power of Jesus

ROBERT W. PAZMIÑO

WIPF & STOCK · Eugene, Oregon

SO WHAT MAKES OUR TEACHING CHRISTIAN?
Teaching in the Name, Spirit, and Power of Jesus

Wipf and Stock Publishers
199 West 8th Avenue, Suite 3
Eugene, Oregon 97401

www.wipfandstock.com

ISBN 13: 978-1-55635-943-9

Library of Congress catalogue number
BV 1464.P39 2008

Manufactured in the U.S.A.

*Dedicated to
Oliver Albert Pazmiño,
my grandson*

Contents

Introduction / *ix*

1   Theological Basics / 1

PART ONE: Teaching in the Name of Jesus / 17

2   Truth and Teaching in the Name of Jesus / 21

3   Love and Teaching in the Name of Jesus / 31

4   Faith and Teaching in the Name of Jesus / 40

5   Hope and Teaching in the Name of Jesus / 47

6   Joy and Teaching in the Name of Jesus / 55

PART TWO: Teaching in the Spirit of Jesus / 65

7   The Spirit Present at Cana / 69

8   The Spirit Present in Contemporary Teaching / 80

PART THREE: Teaching in the Power of Jesus / 93

9   The Power of Jesus in Teaching Insiders and Outsiders / 95

10 The Power of Teaching for Transformation / 107

Conclusion / 119

Bibliography / 121

Index / 125

Introduction

S*O WHAT MAKES OUR Teaching Christian?* I have been dealing with this question in one form or another for the past twenty-seven years of my calling as a professor of Christian education. In other ways I have been dealing with this question from my birth into a Christian family, from my conscious new birth at the age of eighteen when I publicly confessed my faith in Jesus Christ, and upon my commitment to follow him on the occasion of adult baptism. This question takes on increased importance in an age of competing religious claims at the beginning of the third millennium. In answering this question I turn to the scriptural sources that have informed the Christian church and grounded its identity over the centuries. In my case I was particularly attracted to the book of Acts, where with my educational imagination was captured by certain passages when Jesus' followers sought to teach amid opposition. Justo González refers to Acts as the "Gospel of the Spirit," and the first followers of Jesus were empowered by the Spirit as they launched their teaching ministries.[1] I also returned to the exemplary model of Jesus in the Gospel according to John.[2] My first sustained teaching ministry after college, without a published curriculum, was with Hispanic youth in East Harlem, New York. We worked through the gospel of John over three years. The reasons for my attraction to these particular biblical sources will become further apparent in what follows. I believe the question I pose is one that all Christians ought to consider. So what makes our teaching Christian?

In the book of Acts from the first century, following their encounter with the life-transforming teaching of Jesus, Peter and John confronted the Jerusalem Council in relation to their own public ministry of

1. See, *Acts*, 8, where González suggests that the main character of the book is the Holy Spirit.

2. For my overview of Jesus as teacher, see Pazmiño, *God Our Teacher*, 59–86. Besides Jesus' exemplary teaching, Paul is cited for his teaching ministry. See Zuck, *Teaching as Paul Taught*; Osmer, *Teaching Ministry of Congregations*, 3–56; and for my discussion of Paul as teacher, see Pazmiño, "Teachings of Paul," 686–88.

teaching. The passage of Acts 4:1–22 describes how Jesus' first disciples provided a witness in relation to their particular calling to teach. They were proclaiming in Jesus the resurrection of the dead that brought direct opposition from the authorities. The question posed for Jesus' disciples in this first-century drama is one also posed for those who follow Jesus in their teaching ministries today: "By what power or by what name did you do this?" (v. 7). "This" referred to teaching the people in public, as Peter and John so boldly did. The inquiry of the council receives a response from Peter that verse eight notes is preceded by Peter himself being "filled with the Holy Spirit." Peter answered the question about his teaching by referring to the name, spirit, and power of Jesus Christ of Nazareth before the council in Jerusalem. Henri Nouwen in *In the Name of Jesus*, wrestled with Christian distinctives of leadership and noted that "the Christian leader thinks, speaks, and acts in the name of Jesus, who came to free humanity from the power of death and open the way to eternal life."[3]

This work considers the ministry of teaching in the name, spirit, and power of Jesus. To expand upon Peter's words in Acts 4:12, there is no greater name given under heaven by which or whereby teaching can fulfill its highest calling. Part one of this work deals with the question: How can our teaching be like that of Jesus? It suggests that the Christian virtues of truth, love, faith, hope, and joy, all held with humility, serve as guideposts for our teaching in the third millennium. As Christian teachers we can ask ourselves: Are we more in love with God, neighbors, and ourselves in terms of self-care through our teaching? Does our teaching increase the experiences of Christian truth, love, faith, hope, and joy by all participants in our ministries?

In part two, other continuities with Jesus' teaching are explored in relation to the needs of persons that have not radically changed from first-century realities. The spirit of Jesus guides and fills Christian teachers as they respond to the persons they meet, much as Jesus attended to persons at the wedding feast in Cana—the occasion of his first miracle. As Christian teachers we can ask ourselves: What are the real needs of persons and communities in our contexts?

Part three of this work considers how our teaching is empowered by Jesus so that we respond faithfully to both insiders and outsiders in our communities, and invite transformation. Prior to the discussion of each of

3. Nouwen, *Name of Jesus*, 66.

the three parts of this work comes the important consideration of theological basics, presented in chapter one, that serve to anchor the inquiry.

This work is offered with the hope that Christians will engage the call to teach with vision, commitment, and joy. To do less, I suggest, is to dishonor the name, spirit, and power of Jesus in our teaching ministries. I am indebted to one colleague who reviewed my previous work, *God Our Teacher*.[4] In his comments, Dana Wright suggested that this subject be expanded from just the one chapter; that I should write an entire book on Jesus himself in relation to Christian education. Here is the book that Wright encouraged me to write.

I dedicate this work to my grandson, Oliver Albert Pazmiño, with whom I have the privilege of attending church each week. The scriptures in Psalm 128:6 indicate that God blesses the lives of some persons with the opportunity to grandparent. My wife and I have had this blessing these past six years with the birth of our first grandchild. Oliver, along with his parents, lived with us for a month in the past year during a time of transition in their lives. Their transition included a move to a home within a mile from our residence and this delighted the hearts of both sets of grandparents. Time with our grandson has included the usual family-time occasions of holiday celebrations and weekend trips to local attractions for children. But as grandparents, our greatest joy is to sit with Oliver at our local church and to experience, through his eyes, the wonder of worship and the discoveries of the Christian faith that fascinates him in Christian education programs.

One Sunday evening after being present for a children's worship time that morning where youth and adults shared their baptism experiences, Oliver asked me the question: "What is baptism?" His question provided an opportunity to talk about our following and loving Jesus. On another occasion Larisa, my daughter-in-law, shared that Oliver told her that he loved Mindi, the Minister of Christian Education at our church at that time. Here Oliver was affirming the often-repeated Sunday school wisdom: "First I come to love my teacher. Second I come to love my teacher's Bible. Finally I come to love my teacher's Lord." Mindi, a former Christian education student of mine, appreciated hearing the words Oliver was unable to voice in her presence.

4. Pazmiño, *God Our Teacher*.

The blessing of grandparenting is not limited to those who have natural children and grandchildren living close by. It is extended to all who faithfully teach the Christian faith in Sunday schools and various Christian education programs across the globe. Christian teachers equip others to teach who in turn will teach following the pattern of 2 Timothy 2:2 and the exemplary teaching ministry of Jesus. I hope this work may encourage Christian teachers to better follow and represent Jesus in their teaching ministries and practices.

The following personal prayer accompanies this work that I hope will also be the prayer of my readers:

> God our Teacher, we thank you for the opportunity to encourage the faith of others in our natural, faith, and human families. We thank you for the blessing of both seeing and investing in the lives of others that include children, youth, and adults of our own kindred, and neighbors whom we encounter in all the places of our lives. Please help us by your spirit to faithfully teach them, following the example of Jesus, who spoke the truth in love through his actions and words. This we pray in the name, spirit, and power of Jesus the Master Teacher. Amen.

1

Theological Basics

IN EXPLORING THE MINISTRY of teaching in Jesus' name, Christian teachers are dealing with a practical theology. A practical theology deals
with our understanding of God in relation to our actual lives, teaching
ministries, and practices. In bearing the name of Jesus, these ministries
imply a practical Christology, an understanding of the person and work
of Jesus the Christ with implications for the practice of teaching. While
each chapter of this work explores theological basics and connections,
this chapter directly proposes a practical Christology. This chapter considers how Jesus' legacy is played out in the ministries of his followers,
in particular the ministry of teaching. One question emerges in relation
to this chapter: What did Jesus model in his teaching that his followers
today ought to emulate? As Christian teachers we recognize Jesus' unique
person as God's Son and his redemptive work.

In relation to each of the three parts of this work I propose a theological category that helps to both ground and launch consideration of the
Christian ministry of teaching. First, in relation to teaching in the name
of Jesus, the incarnation looms prominent in affirming a sense of identity
for Christian teachers. One's Christian identity centers in one's adoption
as a child of God and one's calling as a follower of Jesus. Second, in relation to teaching in the spirit of Jesus, the crucifixion emerges in inviting
compassion that embraces both suffering and service as a commitment
for Christian teachers. Third, in relation to teaching in the power of Jesus,
the resurrection provides a model for guiding how Christian teachers
consider the possibility of reformation, which invites transformation in
their ministries and in the lives of their students and their wider communities. Therefore the incarnation, crucifixion, and resurrection of Jesus
provide three touchstones for teaching respectively in the name, spirit,
and power of Jesus. These touchstones for Christian teaching provide a

sense of identity, a model for compassion, and an embrace of reformation that Jesus himself modeled in his teaching ministry. The life, death, and resurrection of Jesus are theologically and practically essential to teaching that is Christian in name.

INCARNATION: IDENTITY AND CALLING

By teaching in the name of Jesus, Christians serve, in a representative fashion, their Lord and Savior. Christians bear the name of Christ. They embrace as followers those virtues and values that typified the teaching ministry and life of Jesus. Christian virtues or values need to be incarnated in their own teaching practices. This flows from embracing Jesus' plenipotentiary, or full potential, authority. A plenipotentiary role carries full representative authority and responsibility. Jesus, as incarnate, fully represented God in human form and fully revealed God, even while laying aside his divine privileges. He was fully divine, fully human, and fully one as God's Son who came to earth.[1] The prologue to John's gospel celebrates Jesus' incarnation in John 1:1–18 as the Word of God became flesh and assumed a home in God's creation. John 1:17 declares, "The law indeed was given through Moses; grace and truth came through Jesus Christ." Such a clear declaration of Jesus' identity does not discount any grace or truth coming through Moses, but notes the distinct contributions of Jesus' very person and arrival on earth in human form.

Christian Virtues

To elaborate upon John 1:17, I suggest that along with truth, God's grace in Jesus finds expression in the Christian virtues of faith, hope, love, and joy. These five virtues of truth, faith, hope, love, and joy capture what Christian teachers are called to incarnate in their teaching ministries. They are to faithfully represent their identity as followers of Jesus the Master Teacher. By assuming the name of Jesus and following him as disciples, Christian teachers strive for embodiment, or living out, those virtues that best characterize Jesus and, therefore, represent his essential character. Christian teachers, given their real limitations and sins, do not fully exemplify Jesus in their individual ministries, but they hold this potential in their corpo-

---

1. See Fackre, *Christian Basics*, 44–45, where Jesus is described as "both fully human and fully divine, in inseparable unity" or as the early church said, "Jesus Christ, truly God, truly human and truly one."

rate expressions to be identified as the Body of Christ, as God's children (daughters and sons), and as a household of the Spirit. Henri Nouwen expands upon the importance of our corporate witness:

> I have found it over and over again how hard it is to be truly faithful to Jesus when I am alone. I need brothers and sisters to pray with me, to speak with me about the spiritual task at hand, and to challenge me to stay pure in mind, heart, and body. But far more important, it is Jesus who heals, not I; Jesus who speaks words of truth, not I; Jesus who is Lord, not I. This is very clearly visible when we proclaim the redeeming power of God together. Indeed, whenever we minister together, it is easier for people to recognize that we do not come in our own name, but in the name of the Lord Jesus who sent us.[2]

As Christ's Body, Christians, through diverse teaching ministries, historically and globally bring glory and honor to the name of Jesus. They can also dishonor Jesus' name in their efforts. This, I was reminded, while serving as an academic dean and hearing from students about their experiences with my theological colleagues.

While teaching in a representative fashion in Jesus' name, Christians recognize ways in which their actual practices fail to embody Christian virtues. Both personal practices and corporate designs and structures may fail to uphold the name of Jesus. They often detract from the ideals incarnated in Jesus' ministry. The naming of these real gaps, and the confession of sin by persons and those who represent structures and associations, are necessary for the possibility of more faithful expressions in the present and future. The recognition of the need for change and transformation is also a matter of Jesus' prophetic tradition of teaching.

Jesus, in his own practice, can be seen as a popular prophet in representing the little tradition of agrarian Galilee and of those who stood on the margins of the official great teaching tradition and temple system of his time. The little tradition of Galilee honored the popular culture of the village and common folk, as compared with the elites of the great tradition from Jerusalem.[3] He confronted those patterns of unfaithful practices that were contrary to God's ultimate purposes and intentions for all persons, regardless of their class or standing. This requires of Christian teachers the maintenance of space allowing for disagreement or alterna-

2. Nouwen, *Name of Jesus*, 41.
3. Herzog, *Prophet and Teacher*, 102–9 and 173–76.

tives to what may be advocated, in any particular teaching setting, by those with the authority to teach. Dialogue is crucial that permits those who participate in teaching to voice their responses and thoughts, even if they stand in contrast to the teacher's perspective. The freedom to learn and think requires the extension of choice in teaching practices. This freedom does not discount the wisdom shared by the teacher and the support of necessary forms and discipline required for educational decorum. Forms and discipline can, in practice, support the dialogue and freedom required for the ownership of learning by persons who sit or journey with their teachers. This presents a paradox and tension for Christian teachers, but a necessary one.

Paradoxes

The amazing paradox suggested by the incarnation itself is that Christian teachers are called to incarnate in their ministries the very presence of Jesus Christ. Just as Jesus incarnated God in his very earthly presence, Christian teachers are to represent the very life and spirit of Jesus in their persons and teaching practices. This is a high calling, and worthy of the most diligent and receptive of Christians, to abide in Christ as Christ graciously abides by his spirit in the lives of believers. This reality fulfills Jesus' prayer as recorded in John 17:20–23:

> As you, Father, are in me and I in you, may they also be in us, so that the world may believe that you have sent me. The glory that you have given me I have given them, so that they may be one, as we are one, I in them and you in me, that they may become completely one, so that the world may know that you have sent me and have loved them even as you have loved me.

This amazing paradox is also a glorious one where Jesus is made present through the faithful teaching ministries of his disciples in a representative way. In this process Christian teachers recognize the gaps, dysfunctions, and discrepancies in their own lives and ministries. Nevertheless, at their best, Christian teachers rely upon the spirit of Jesus Christ to correct and transcend those gaps, known theologically as sin, in order to represent the living Christ in their ministries.

The desire to better represent Jesus is based upon God's love made manifest in Jesus. The apostle Paul captures this perspective in sharing with the Philippian Christians: "Christ will be exalted in my body,

4

whether by life or by death. For to me, living is Christ and dying is gain"
(Phil 1:20b–21). According to Paul's life motto, living in a teaching ministry is Christ where Christ is seen through the faithful efforts of a Christian
teacher. Paul, in this same letter, suggests additional insights regarding
this mystery in admonishing the beloved believers: "work out your own
salvation with fear and trembling; for it is God who is at work in you, en-
abling you both to will and to work for his good pleasure" (Phil 2:12b–13).
Christian teachers' strivings are complemented by reliance upon God's
gracious working within them to accomplish divine purposes. This divine
working embraces the paradoxes of life and death, and both divine and
human efforts with their roots in the incarnation.

For Christian teachers the incarnation suggests presence and availability, just as God is made present in the person of Jesus. Such a presence
and availability is in a way that is representative of Jesus. Representing
Jesus is an awesome challenge that implies both responsibility and privilege. Christian teachers are responsible to be good stewards of their gifts
for teaching. Christian teachers are privileged to have access to the all
that the triune God intends for humanity, with God as the educator of
all creation, Jesus as the exemplar for teaching practice, and the Holy
Spirit as ever-present partner in one's calling to teach. This accessibility
follows from a full appreciation of what God has accomplished in Jesus'
incarnation.

Christ's incarnated life finds further expression in the faithful ministries of Christian teachers. Teachers rely upon God's Spirit graciously
working both within and despite them, sometimes in a paradoxical way.[4]
Standing in the tradition of Jesus and following Jesus as disciples calls
for honoring, in faithful ways, what Jesus modeled and taught. If Jesus
can serve effectively as an exemplar, that I have proposed in my previous
writings, Christian teachers must attend to those virtues that most cohere
with his teaching practices. I identify five Christian virtues for teaching,
namely love, faith, hope, joy, and truth. In one setting where I taught on

4. For a discussion of God's working in, through, and despite Christian teachers, see
Pazmiño, *God Our Teacher*, chapters 2, 4, and 5. Chapter 3 of that work explores the topic
of God, with us in the person and work of Jesus, who serves as an exemplar for Christian
teaching.

this topic, one participant proposed the additional virtue of humility to my lineup.[5]

Humility

Humility can serve to identify the ways in which Christians embrace any virtues and how they are shared with others. Humility implies that if Christian teachers are actually incarnating Christ-like virtues, these are communicated or taught to others in implicit, rather then explicit, ways. Humility is the receptive stance of open hands and hearts that Christians maintain in relation to virtues that are gifts of God. Christians hold these virtues in the earthen or clay vessels of their human bodies (2 Cor 4:1–15, especially v. 7). Christian teachers can celebrate the expression of virtues incarnated in the life and ministry of Jesus; these virtues are worthy to emulate. But teachers are not to bring attention to themselves as paragons of virtue. Humility reminds Christian teachers of the ever-present danger of arrogant self-righteousness in teaching. Humility can be explored in relation to pride. False pride is preoccupied with being better than others, whereas genuine pride considers one's gifts and works in relation to God's particular, personal, and public call to teach.[6]

Genuine humility affirms the self as created by God and worthy, whereas false humility distorts that self either in an exaggerated or a diminished manner. Genuine pride and humility follows from Christians embracing their identity as children of God, disciples of Jesus, and partners of the Holy Spirit in their teaching ministries. Paul suggested this in Romans 12:3: "For by the grace given to me I say to everyone among you not to think of yourself more highly than you ought to think, but to think with sober judgment, each according to the measure of faith that God has assigned." The complementary advice would be not to think of yourself lowlier than you ought to think. Genuine pride and humility lead to self-care and self-affirmation. Such a response does not deteriorate into self-hate or self-love that excludes God and others. Self-hate and self-love that exclude God fail to obey Jesus' two great commandments to love God and neighbor.

5. Roger White of the Haggard School of Theology, Azusa Pacific University, shared this insight at Talbot Theological Seminary, La Mirada, California, on January 5, 2005, during a symposium I led on the theme of this book.

6. See my discussion of genuine and false pride in Pazmiño, *By What Authority?*, 74–75. John R. W. Scott has a helpful article, "Am I supposed to love?," 27–28.

Admission and confession are implied in identifying humility as a necessary stance in exploring Christian virtues. As Christians we admit our failings and confess our sins before a loving and forgiving God. This does not imply a quick rush to grace, but a sober assessment of what teachers hope others might imitate in our examples of living. As Christians we also admit our gifts and the fruits of our ministry as blessed by God. The apostle Paul suggests such, as noted in 1 Corinthians 11:1: "Be imitators of me, as I am of Christ." The importance of the "as" is very apparent to disciples of Jesus as they journey through this life and strive to represent their Lord in the ministries of teaching. Why is this the case?

Christian teachers recognize the unique ministry of Jesus as the Son of God who is the fullest revelation of God in human flesh and form. Any claims to Christian perfection, this side of death and new life, can be suspect in the light of the virtue of humility, from my understanding of sin that affects the current human situation. The writer to the Hebrews makes a clear distinction in relation to Jesus: "For we do not have a high priest who is unable to sympathize with our weaknesses, but we have one who in every respect has been tested as we are, yet without sin" (Heb 4:15). Jesus' earthly journey included his being tempted in a host of ways without succumbing to sin. This enables him to identify with the real weaknesses and failings of Christian teachers to fulfill God's purposes in living out the virtues and ideals that are essential to the Christian faith. But Christian teachers have hope, with the outrageous mercy and grace of God made available in Jesus Christ and made effectual in the ministry of the Holy Spirit. This is good news for teachers and students alike as a means by which to fulfill God's call to holiness and justice in life and all forms of education. These forms include formal, nonformal, and informal educational efforts in a variety of Christian education ministries.[7]

There is hope for parents in homes, teachers in schools, pastors and teachers in congregations, lay and clerical ministers in friendships, mentors in relationships, and persons in any educational encounters where the name of Jesus is both honored and claimed. Where human teachers fail and confess their failings, God's grace and forgiveness can address the gap and invite a hopeful change in future efforts. Jesus' unique redemptive purpose and divine powers, though laid aside in his earthly incarnation, distinguish his earthly ministry from that of his followers.

7. See Pazmiño, *Principles and Practices*, 61–65, for definitions of formal, nonformal, and informal approaches toward Christian education.

Identity and Practices

The book of Acts 2:42–47 describes the activities or practices that the followers of Jesus instituted in their times together following the birth of the Christian Church. Acts 2:42 notes: "They devoted themselves to the apostle's teaching and fellowship, to the breaking of bread and the prayers." The order of their activities is noteworthy. Teaching comes first, followed by fellowship, the breaking of bread, and prayers, all of which suggest corporate worship. Identifying with Jesus leads to these faith practices following Jesus' departure from the earth. Jesus' followers incarnate their faith and identify with him in their life together.

While recognizing Jesus' unique ministry and their own real limitations, Christian teachers celebrate their identity as those graciously called by God to represent Jesus in their lives and ministries. This is a high calling that requires a daily and hourly reliance in prayer upon the resources made available to believers. The preeminent resource is the spirit of Christ gifted to Jesus' followers upon his departure from the earth. The spirit extends Jesus' ministry begun in the incarnation and waiting fulfillment at the Second Coming of Jesus to earth. The actual hope of Jesus' return serves as a motivation for holy living and faithful representation of those virtues Jesus honored in his journey and teaching ministry (1 John 3:2–3). That earthly journey ended abruptly with his crucifixion, though this experience was not his final legacy in his life of service and compassion on behalf of humankind and all creation. Part one of this work considers the outworking of the incarnation in relation to the Christian virtues of truth, love, faith, hope, and joy. Christian teachers who seek to teach in Jesus' name hold these virtues with a sense of humility. Christian teaching confronts the reality of death as experienced by Jesus in his crucifixion.

CRUCIFIXION: COMPASSION AND SERVICE

The crucifixion of Jesus represents a model for Christian teachers in terms of compassion and service capturing the spirit of Jesus in relation to teaching. Compassion denotes the willingness to suffer with other persons as motivated by love. By entering into the suffering of others, Christians embrace the suffering of Jesus Christ. In Jesus' case this suffering extended beyond suffering *with* to include suffering *for* other persons. The crucifixion is proclamation of God's great love in Jesus reaching out to all. Jesus certainly humbled himself in initially taking on human form at his birth. But the extent of his compassion for persons is evident in the passion narratives with his willingness subject himself to a "show trial" in Jerusalem and its verdict of death upon a cross.[8] Incarnation required an encounter with human suffering and the depth of sin to realize a remedy made available in Jesus' crucifixion. The scandal of this event and the efficacy of his willing sacrifice to end all sacrifices demonstrate the extent of his loving service in fulfilling God's purposes. Christians affirm this reality in their understanding of Jesus' atonement. The cross calls for a confrontation with suffering in the world, recognizing that suffering was embraced in God through Jesus' passion.

The agony and shame of the crucifixion has been captured in various media including the much-publicized film, "The Passion of the Christ." On a personal level, my first time viewing of that particular film occurred while I was also cooking a meal in my home. In a rush to return to the living room viewing, and while roasting potatoes in oil, I managed to burn my arm to the second degree. Additional treatment of an infection of the arm meant that I missed the opening session of a faculty retreat the next day. During this timeslot my colleagues voted for me *in absentia* to serve as the faculty marshal who coordinates public events for the school. Jesus' passion portrayed on the screen is therefore closely associated in my experience with my own bodily suffering and service in teaching. I do question the compassion of my teaching colleagues in voting for me in my injured state, but that is another matter. Actually my service as faculty marshal was a prelude to my later serving as the interim dean of the faculty for a year and a half. I do not associate service as an academic dean with a crucifixion, though any leadership calling involves both suffering and joy in the life of a faith community. Well beyond any personal suffering experienced by Christians, the crucifixion calls for a recognition of the suffering experienced by humanity and all of creation, and solidarity with those who suffer.

The scriptures teach that Jesus willingly accepted his death upon the cross to fulfill God's plans. John's gospel repeats this theme. As the good

---

8. For a discussion of the "show trial" of Jesus, see Herzog, *Prophet and Teacher*, 216–27. "A show trial is one way of processing deviants in an authoritarian society," in which "the guilt of the person to be tried has already been determined, usually on political grounds," and its purpose is "not only to execute a subversive but to publicly shame and humiliate an enemy of the state so as to discredit and degrade everything he represents (216)."

shepherd, Jesus' teaching is noted: "I lay down my life for the sheep" (John 10:15). This chapter in John elaborates upon this teaching of the good shepherd and his ministry with the sheep, with his followers and friends:

> For this reason the Father loves me, because I lay down my life in order to take it up again. No one takes it from me, but I lay it down of my own accord. I have power to lay it down, and I have power to take it up again. I received this command from my Father. (John 10:17–18)

This theme is echoed in John 15:13–14 where following Jesus' claim to be the true vine and source of joy for those who abide in him notes: "No one has greater love than this, to lay down one's life for one's friends. You are my friends if you do what I command you." Christian teachers follow Jesus as his sheep, friends, and followers, embracing his example of service and love or compassion. This loving service is related to a stance of obedience in relation to God's call and command. That call and command may come through burnt arms and colleagues' votes less dramatically than a crucifixion, nevertheless requiring a life of service. One major proviso in noting the crucifixion is to celebrate the reality that Jesus' sacrifice of his very life ends the cycle of sacrificial suffering required for God's forgiveness and grace in relation to humanity that awaits the full redemption of creation. The motivation of love, and not appeasement, is to guide service in the light of God's great gift of Jesus, his Son, who fulfilled God's plan as the lamb slain or slaughtered from the foundation of the world (Rev 13:8).

The accounts of the crucifixion in the gospel of John include Jesus' appearance before the recognized Roman authority, Pilate. Pilate presents a haunting question to Jesus in his show trial: "What is truth?" (John 18:38).[9] This question in part is answered by Jesus' astounding willingness to so deeply love humanity by laying down his life in service. Truth finds expression in God's compassion for persons that is captured in the often repeated verse of John 3:16: "For God so loved the world that he gave his only Son, so that everyone who believes in him may not perish but may have eternal life."

---

9. See chapter 6, "Authority of Truth in an Age of Pluralism," Pazmiño, *By What Authority?*, 119–46.

Christian Teachers' Love

What can Christian teachers in turn give to their students as expressions of the depth of their love or compassion? Their dedication and diligence in the ministry of teaching finds expression in the three phases of teaching, namely preparation, instruction, and evaluation.[10] In many settings, teaching is not a valued ministry or profession. Despite the external values associated with other ministries or professions, teaching provides a distinctive opportunity to invest one's life in the rising generations, or any generations, open to and excited about the possibility of learning together. The passing on and exploration of wisdom is essential to the continuity, growth, and transformation of human communities, including that community identified as the Christian Church in its various expressions.

Teaching in the spirit of Jesus' compassion and service raises the matter of the essential ethos of his teaching. This ethos, referring to the tone or quality of Jesus' teaching, modeled a moment-to-moment reliance upon God in response to human need guided by love. The pattern evident with this ethos is found in Jesus' interaction at the wedding of Cana. Jesus joined the feast and was one with the wedding guests, along with his disciples. Jesus was also an individual in terms of his actions not determined by his mother's urgent request. Jesus was conscious of the timing of his ministry. His actions of supplying the need for wine exemplified his love that eventuated in the shedding of his blood and the giving of his body upon the cross. This compassionate service is recalled in the repeated celebration of his table fellowship in the Christian community. Teaching in the spirit of Jesus calls for welcoming others; it calls for learning, sharing, and worshipping with them.

The pattern of table fellowship is repeated in Luke's gospel with the encounter on the road to Emmaus (Luke 24:13–35). The first miracle at Cana sets the pattern that is prominent in the crucifixion. It is also renewed in the shared meal on the road waiting the final fulfillment of the marriage supper of the lamb, which is described in the book of Revelation (Rev 19:1–10). Christians reenact this table fellowship when they celebrate the Lord's Supper, and I suggest whenever Christian teachers share the fruits of learning with others in the spirit and name of Jesus. This suggests that teaching itself, and the accompanying learning, are sacramental acts in the sense of being a means of God's grace gifted to humanity.

10. I develop a description of faithful teaching in Pazmiño, *Basics of Teaching*.

Part two of this work considers teaching in the spirit of Jesus with a detailed theological look at his first miracle at the wedding of Cana that prefigures his crucifixion, and also at the table fellowship made possible by his death with his life's blood substituting for the water changed into wine. The promise of the crucifixion and its efficacy is realized in Jesus' resurrection. Resurrection follows from the crucifixion. Resurrection cannot be separated from the reality of the cross and what God's love accomplished through Jesus' life and death. The cross and Jesus' crucifixion remains a memorial for the extensive love that Jesus calls his followers to consider in their teaching ministries. The book of Hebrews describes this reality in chapter 12, verse 2: "looking to Jesus the pioneer and perfecter of our faith, who for the sake of the joy that was set before him endured the cross, disregarding its shame, and has taken his seat at the right hand of the throne of God." Near the front door to my home, a plaque is set on the wall that displays a cross with the word "joy" emblazed under it. The joy set before Jesus finds expression in his resurrection.

RESURRECTION: REFORMATION AND TRANSFORMATION

Teaching in the power of Jesus is often explored in the light of what occurred in Jesus' earthly journey after his crucifixion. As noted above in exploring the crucifixion from John 10:18b, Jesus is recorded as saying: "I have power to lay it [referring to his life] down, and I have power to take it up again." The crucifixion involved the laying down of his life and the resurrection involved his taking it up again. Power is manifested in each action, though most Christians associate power with the resurrection more than the crucifixion. Nevertheless, the crucifixion can be associated with the power of both love and service. I find it noteworthy that Paul described the motto of his life in terms of both the crucifixion and resurrection in writing to the Christians he taught in Philippi: "I want to know Christ and the power of his resurrection and the sharing of his sufferings by becoming like him in his death, if somehow I may attain the resurrection from the dead" (Phil 3:10–11). Glimpses of both the crucifixion and resurrection are found in Jesus' teaching ministry prior to the historical events of Passion Week described vividly in the Gospels.

Two prototypical encounters with Jesus are found in his tutorials in the gospel of John with both the Samaritan woman and Nicodemus, where transformation so desperately sought is found in distinct time sequences. These events prior to both the crucifixion and resurrection as the great acts of Jesus' atoning work are a better parallel for the potential of Christian teachers in their ministries. John 1:10–13 introduces the theme of transformation from this opening prologue to the gospel that describes Jesus' ministry on earth:

> He was in the world, and the world came into being through him; yet the world did not know him. He came to what was his own, and his own people did not accept him. But to all who received him, who believed in his name, he gave power to become children of God, who were born, not of blood or of the will of the flesh or of the will of man, but of God.

The words "Power to become the children of God" suggest a process of transformation that follows from believing in Jesus' name and receiving him, as Nicodemus did over time and the Samarian woman in a shorter span of time. Power is experienced by having life in Jesus' name and in being born of God. Being born of God is the invitation that is both explicit and implicit in Jesus' teaching and is extended to the teaching ministries of his disciples. These two persons encountered Jesus from different ends of the socioeconomic spectrum. A hunger exists for transformation at all levels of society and in all areas of human and created life. The dynamics may vary whether one is an outsider or insider of any particular human community.

To be treated as an outsider, as "the other," in any human encounter can deny one's personhood. Those viewed as the others are expendable. When survival is threatened, the other is most vulnerable. Martin Buber in his work *I and Thou* explores the importance of recognizing the personhood of all "others."[11] The openness to transformation can be radically different for outsiders as compared with insiders. Jesus made outsiders insiders within his fellowship and on occasion insiders outsiders in paradoxical ways. Jesus himself an outsider beyond his Galilean context could identify with those of outsider status in his first-century world. For outsiders the longed-for transformation may be viewed as an event, compared with the process for insiders who have much to lose or relinquish in leaving the center and coming to the margins. Jesus' teaching models a Galilean principle.

11. Buber, *I and Thou*.

The Galilean principle affirms our huddling with God and God's people to form a clear sense of identity as God's children (emerging from the incarnation) complemented by our mixing with the diversity of humanity represented by those who stand on the margins of any community or society (emerging from the crucifixion and resurrection).[12] The perspective of Jesus from Galilee extends to include Calvary and Easter day with a stop along the way in Samaria. The incarnation "makes possible the continuing tasks of the Galilean teacher who rescues us from untruth, the Calvary savior who delivers us from sin, and the Easter liberator who overcomes suffering and death."[13] In John 3, Jesus himself the outsider, is at the religious center of Jerusalem and his transformative invitation to Nicodemus is issued at night and in private conversation. Whereas, in John 4, Jesus' invitation to the Samaritan came in the light of day and in the public setting of the village well where all later meet. At the well Jesus, as the Jewish male, is the insider and the Samaritan woman is the outsider. The irony of the accounts is that Jesus and the Samaritan woman have a private encounter in such a public space. A study of the contrasts between Nicodemus and the Samaritan woman, both whose lives are transformed by the power of Jesus' teaching and the offer of new life, is found in part three of this work.

The case studies in teaching of Nicodemus and the Samaritan woman in part three serve to deepen an appreciation of how transformation is possible in teaching both by way of an event and a process. The effectual reach of Jesus' power is extended through his resurrection and the new life offered to those who receive him and embrace his teaching for all of life. Resurrection is evident over time in Nicodemus' life as a process and, quite suddenly, in the case of the Samaritan woman as an event. Resurrection emerged from the interpersonal encounters with Jesus that are peppered with the posing of questions. Primarily, Nicodemus and the Samaritan woman pose questions as they search for truth. But we also discover that Jesus himself poses questions in his conversations. Resurrection makes possible a new truth that leads to new life.

---

12. See Pazmiño, *God Our Teacher*, 13, 62, 64, 84, 86, 116, 132, and 149, for a discussion of the Galilean principle related to Christian teaching.

13. Fackre, *Christian Basics*, 52.

CONCLUDING PRACTICAL THOUGHTS

The search for a practical Christology celebrates the theological basics of Jesus' incarnation, crucifixion, and resurrection as essentials for Christian teaching. As Steve Kang notes in describing truth-embodying communities in which "the life, death and resurrection of Jesus Christ are celebrated and continue to shape the way of life of its people through the power of the Holy Spirit,"[14] Christian teachers support the formation and growth of such communities as they consider with their students what is required of us.

The incarnation requires Christian teachers to embrace our humanity and identity as followers and disciples of Jesus. We ask ourselves what virtues do we actually live out and incarnate in our lives and teaching practices. The matter of virtues relates to our character and what others see in us with the potential of reflecting Christ. The living out of Christian virtues serves to honor our adoption as God's children and our calling as Jesus' disciples. Jesus' disciples fulfill what Micah 6:8 suggests is crucial in living: "O mortal, what is good; and what does the Lord require of you but to do justice, and to love kindness, and to walk humbly with your God?"

The crucifixion requires Christian teachers to admit our lacks and shortcomings for which Christ himself is God's remedy. We also address the reality of suffering and struggle that is a part of the human condition. The spirit of Christ is one of compassion and service in the midst of the sin, death, and loss that persons confront. The restoration of joy is symbolized in the water now transformed into wine. Jesus' provision embodies a new covenant and relationship beyond the potential shame of no more wine to serve others. Jesus' provision is made evident at the cross that despite the brokenness and death offers God's amazing grace to fill human need with persons embraced as God's beloved. The water for cleansing is replaced with the wine of fulfillment with the best saved for last, contrary to all expectations and surprising all with joy.

The resurrection requires Christian teachers to deal with the invitation of reformation and transformation viewed as both event and process. This invitation comes in the seasonal and liturgical years of faith communities and in the personal rhythms of the years, as exemplified in the lives of Nicodemus and the Samaritan woman that Christian tradition names Photini. The pace of change varies in each of their cases because the sea-

14. Kang, "Truth-Embodying Households," 48.

sons of our lives vary with the pilgrim. Resurrection affirms that there is a time to live, a time to die, and a time to live again as God graciously works through the transitions and surprises of our earthly journeys. Teaching can provide occasions to reflect upon God's presence in all of life, across the span of years from birth to death to second birth, as Nicodemus learned at night and the Samaritan woman in the heat of the day.

So what makes for teaching in the name, spirit, and power of Jesus? Christians who teach are invited to explore this question in what follows with theological basics in hand and heart.

PART ONE

Teaching in the Name of Jesus

O N ONE OF OUR yearly auto trips from Massachusetts to Florida for a visit with my mother-in-law, my wife Wanda and I had the opportunity to visit the mission of *Nombre de Diós* in Saint Augustine. For years, in passing the road sign, I wondered what that name might mean. In visiting, I learned that on September 8, 1565, Pedro Menendez de Aviles landed on that site to found Saint Augustine, which was the first permanent Christian settlement in what became the United States. Though not noted in my elementary and secondary school textbooks, Saint Augustine was settled prior to Plymouth Rock in Massachusetts, my home state, and Jamestown in Virginia.[1] The Spanish pioneers named this landing "*Nombre de Diós*," (Name of God), in honor of the *holy name* of Jesus. What about that holy and precious name of Jesus in relation to the ministries of Christian teaching in the third millennium? We are living about 440 years after that first landing and I wonder how honoring and bearing the holy name of Jesus can make a difference in how we teach today and in the future.

As a teacher with a calling to think about and practice teaching in the Christian faith, I am fascinated with how the scriptures describe the ministry of teaching. Christian teaching is described as teaching "in the name of Jesus." The phrase "in the name of Jesus" appears in a number of New or Second Testament passages and is associated with a variety of activities.[2] Those activities include coming and leading (Matt 24:5),

1. González, *Mañana*, 31.

2. The designation Second Testament for the New Testament can avoid a pejorative association with the Old Testament that some Jewish scholars associate with the Christian naming of their scriptures. Common Christian use refers to the New Testament that honors the Old Testament as suggested by Matthew 13:52 in relation to teaching or scribal tradition that honors the treasure of the old as well as the new. Old in a pejorative sense may be more associated with the ageism that exists in U.S. culture that can be confronted by Christians and Jews.

praying or asking (John 14:13, 14; 15:16; 16:23–24, 26), proclaiming (Luke 24:47; Acts 8:12), speaking or preaching (Acts 9:27), glorifying (Rev 15:4), gathering (Matt 18:20), receiving or welcoming (Matt 18:5), bearing or bringing (Acts 9:15), prophesying (Matt 7:22), praising (Acts 19:17), healing (Acts 3:6), believing (John 20:31), baptizing (Matt 28:19), anointing (Jas 5:14), casting out demons (Mark 9:38; Luke 9:49), living (John 20:31), dying (Acts 21:13), and also teaching (Acts 4:18; 5:28). As Christians we are called to do all of our ministries in the name of Jesus. I wonder what teaching in the name of Jesus might mean for Christians in both the first and now third millennia.

To do something in the name of another person assumes one has authority and that one is serving in a representative way—in a plenipotentiary manner. Teaching on behalf of Jesus or invoking his name is both an awesome responsibility and a distinct privilege. The responsibility is strikingly noted in James 3:1: "Not many of you should become teachers, my brothers and sisters, for you know that we who teach will be judged with greater strictness." How do we embody or incarnate Jesus' manner of teaching in concrete ways? The privilege is suggested in Matthew 28:18–20 which can be viewed as an educational commission. This commission promises Jesus' authority, power, and presence in making disciples and teaching them to obey everything Jesus commanded. Teaching others to obey everything Jesus commanded is a life-long and joyous task.

Teaching in the name of Jesus is noted in the accounts of Luke and Acts that describe the ministry of Jesus' disciples (Luke 24:47; Acts 4:17–18; 5:28, 40), if one includes both preaching and teaching in the proclamation of the gospel, as I do. Raymond Abba, in describing the meaning of a name, indicates that in "biblical thought a name is not a mere label of identification; it is an expression of the essential nature of its bearer."[3]

What is it to bear the name of Jesus in our teaching as with other ministry activities? As Christians, we have been called, saved, baptized, authorized, enlivened, and empowered by the name and person of Jesus. Bearing or reflecting the image of Jesus in our teaching seems like an amazing and even overwhelming task. To invoke the name of Jesus in our teaching is a responsibility and privilege implying both a major obligation and an abundant blessing. Colossians 3:17 sets the standard for all our activities as Christians: "And whatever you do, in word or deed, do

---

3. Abba, "Name," 500.

everything in the name of the Lord Jesus, giving thanks to God the Father through him." Teaching and learning are included in the "whatever" noted here.

Bearing the name of Jesus in our teaching should reveal his essential nature in some specific ways. I suggest that those specific ways can reflect the Christian virtues that Jesus manifested in his earthly teaching that set a clear example for us. These five virtues are truth, faith, hope, love, and joy. They are associated with the following paired callings: truth, a call for integrity; love, a call for care; faith, a call for action; hope, a call for courage; and joy, a call for celebration.[4] The five chapters of part one explore teaching in Jesus' name in relation to these five Christian virtues that serve to distinguish Christian teaching. My discussion of these virtues begins with truth and love following the biblical injunction, "to speak the truth in love" (Eph 4:15), that directly applies to the ministry of teaching. These five virtues represent five gems that can adorn our teaching ministry in the name and service of Jesus Christ. This service is a high calling that deserves the best efforts of his followers until the consummation of his return to earth. Until that day the Holy Spirit has been sent to partner with Christians in their teaching ministries. A wide diversity of teaching ministries characterizes the Christian Church today and I imagine into eternity.

Abba, in analyzing acting in the name of Jesus, suggests that it first denotes participation in his authority (Mark 9:38; 16:17; 1 Cor 5:4; Jas 5:14) and on his behalf, which is clearly affirmed in Matthew 28:18–20 in relation to teaching.[5] Second, it also suggests consciously invoking the name of Jesus and relying upon his presence and power (Acts 9:27, 29).[6] Therefore both a receptive resting upon Jesus' authority and an active seeking out his empowerment points up the need for reliance upon prayer in teaching. A third suggestion found in accounts from John's gospel (John 14:14; 15:16; 16:23–24, 26) refer to "being rooted in Christ," "prompted by the mind of Christ and in accordance with his character" and will.[7] These characteristics apply to anointed Christian teaching in

---

4. I describe the values or virtues modeled in Jesus' teaching in Pazmiño, *God Our Teacher*, 76–78.

5. See my discussion of authority and power related to teaching in Pazmiño, *By What Authority?*

6. Abba, "Name," 507.

7. Ibid., 507.

proportion to what the apostle Paul notes in relation to his own ministry in 1 Corinthians 11:1: "Be imitators of me, as I am of Christ." The extent to which the Christian teacher is rooted in Christ and reflecting Jesus' mind, character, and will, her or his teaching and life are worthy of imitation. A fourth suggestion from Abba refers to relying upon Jesus as a source of authority, devotion, and acting directly for his sake (Matt 18:5; 24:5; Luke 24:47; Acts 3:16; 4:17–18; 5:28, 40). Reliance upon Jesus' authority results in direct public appeals and actions being made and claimed in his name. Pastors make this explicit as they officiate at a baptism, communion service, or marriage worship service. But all believers, including teachers who use their gifts and services, are to make this connection. All of one's life, both public and personal, holds the potential for teaching others. This active invoking of the power and authority of Jesus' name[8] assumes a level of corporate accountability and sanction. For Christian teachers this requires a commitment to the Christian faith while being a loving critic of both the church and wider society in being faithful to Jesus.

Teaching in the name of Jesus calls for careful reflection and faithful practice in the third millennium as much as it did in the first millennium. The five Christian virtues of truth, love, faith, hope, and joy provide touchstones to guide teachers in their ministries in order to faithfully fulfill their calling with humility.

---

8. Ibid.

2

Truth and Teaching in the Name of Jesus

THEOLOGICAL ANCHORS FOR TRUTH

THE MATTER OF TRUTH is central and crucial to the ministry of teaching. The search for truth undergirds the process of teaching and the outcomes sought in learning. In the Christian faith the search for truth engages God's wisdom, as revealed in Jesus Christ himself, "in whom are hidden as the treasures of wisdom and knowledge" (Col 2:3). With the rise of postmodernism today, the outcomes proposed by any search for truth have been subject to question in relation to the Christian claims of universal truth. This cultural and epistemological shift runs counter to the historic claims of the Christian faith as revealing universal truth for all times and persons.

While claiming universality the Christian faith has, paradoxically, celebrated the place of particularity made most explicit in the incarnation of Jesus of Nazareth. Indeed, Christian faith embraces the scandal of particularity in God assuming human form in the person of a first-century Galilean Jewish carpenter. Postmodern shifts provide the occasion to celebrate the particular embedded nature of each person and context along with distinctive truths disclosed, discerned, and discovered by searching for truth. At the same time, these shifts result in a deep hunger for community and relationship in the lives of the rising generations. This also is the case for those experiencing fragmentation with the loss of an integrative wholeness in life. In the anguish of this postmodern dilemma, Christians claim that in Jesus Christ and his teachings, persons can find an answer to their longings for truth that provides perspective for our particular individual lives and our most public selves with universal longings. While providing an answer, the Christian faith still represents foolishness and a stumbling block to many in wider society (1 Cor 1:18–31).

Jesus as a human person offers to an estranged humanity insights into the souls and very spirits of persons. Jesus in his person embodies a new humanity who is both radically open to God and in relationship with all his earthly neighbors embedded in the totality of creation. The means for persons to discover their true selves is suggested in the two great commandments that Jesus explicitly taught. Loving God with all of one's heart, soul, mind, and strength is the first of the commandments (Luke 10:27). This first commandment orients persons regarding their true origin, identity, and destiny. The great questions of the human mind and spirit: Where did I come from? What am I? Where am I going?, find their answers in God. The great Tahitian painting of Paul Gaughan portrays these questions visually and that work is known as his masterpiece. In observing that painting, one can see a church with a cross atop its steeple that suggests a place to find answers to these persistent human questions in the cross of Jesus Christ. Persons are created in the very image of God (Gen 1:27) and, as God's creatures, are accountable to fulfill God's purposes for all of creation. Persons find their primary identity as children of God, and potentially friends and followers of Jesus Christ, and vessels or a temple of the Holy Spirit in the world. This radical (going to the roots) grounding makes all the difference in one's life journey fulfilling a particular calling or vocation. The perspective of one's ultimate destiny from the vantage point of Christian faith is in eternal communion with God as the source of all of life, including life after death.

With these theological anchors for a life journey, Christians search for truth that provides purpose and ultimate meaning both within and beyond the contours of our earthly existence. Abundant life can be experienced in the present. Our present life also finds hope of its eternal expression in the providential care of God. Truth and its human search in teaching and learning find their resting place in the ultimate grounding provided by God. God created the human mind, body, and spirit. Restless and curious persons, groups, communities, and societies find their immediate and ultimate rest in God.[1] The resting of our hearts, souls, spirits, and minds can be found in the person, life, and ministry of Jesus Christ. This is the good news that Christian teachers share. Christians also

1. My thoughts expand upon the thoughts of Augustine of Hippo: "our hearts are restless until they find their rest in You," found in Augustine, *Augustine's Confessions*, 1.

humbly recognize their limited understanding of the truth and the need for a life long search being dependent upon God's wisdom.

THE SPIRIT OF JESUS CHRIST

Jesus' presence is extended today through the person and ministry of the Holy Spirit who is also identified as the very spirit of Christ (Rom 8:9; Gal 4:6) gifted to Jesus' disciples and followers (John 20:22; Acts 1:8; 2:1–13). The Holy Spirit is also identified as the Spirit of Truth (John 14:17; 15:26; 1 John 4:6; 5:6) whom Jesus identified: "When the Spirit of truth comes, he will guide you into all truth" (John 16:13). Such a promise has far reaching implications and obligations for teaching in the name of Jesus. It suggests that teaching itself should be seen as a spiritual ministry requiring spiritual gifts. It suggests that the Spirit's guidance accessed through prayer, study, loving dialogue, and reflection upon life itself is crucial for the discernment of truth. It suggests that openness to the Spirit's wisdom and revelation by teachers calls for an honoring of the variety of ways in which God's Spirit has worked in the past, works in the present, and will work in the future. The popular media regularly raises spiritual themes in films like "The Matrix."

Personally this truth about the Spirit has involved for me an insight shared by my colleague Julie Gorman. Gorman pointed out that God's Spirit does not only speak through my words as a teacher in teaching encounters with others.[2] The Holy Spirit can speak very effectively through the insights shared by others. Allowing and calling for the speech of others through dialogue can allow the Spirit's wisdom to be shared beyond any thoughts in my notes or lesson plans. As Christian teachers we can ask ourselves whether we allow for a community of truth to be practiced in our teaching by offering our teaching with open hands instead of pointed fingers. Parker Palmer suggests that "to teach is to create a space in which the community of truth is practiced."[3] Peer learning is an important feature in any educational opportunity. As with the thoughts and comments of any teachers, the insights shared by others calls for spiritual discernment. Spiritual discernment is fostered through a conscious and

---

2. Personal conversation with Gorman at Fuller Theological Seminary, Pasadena, CA, July 27, 2000.

3. Palmer, *Know As We Are Known*, xii.

prayerful reliance upon the Holy Spirit in the preparation, instruction, and evaluation phases of teaching.[4]

THE AUTHORITY OF TEACHING

The matter of truth raises the important question of the authority of one's teaching. This question was one that was raised directly with Jesus in his earthly ministry (Luke 20:1–8). What distinguished Jesus' teaching from his contemporaries was noted as his teaching with authority and this brought with it a sense of amazement (Mark 1:22). In the search for truth occasioned by teaching and learning, the matter of one's sources for truth is subject to scrutiny as was the case for Jesus.[5] The Christian tradition through its Wesleyan roots has identified the four sources as scripture, tradition, reason, and experience. Given the challenge of separating reason from experience, the theologian Gabriel Fackre proposes three basic tests of authority: scripture as the *source*, church tradition as the *resource*, and experience of the world as the *setting*.[6] These three tests of authority can not only guide the search of Christian truth, but also serve to provide the parameters used for discerning truth within the efforts of teaching and learning. Christians affirm that scripture provides the primary source for truth about God and life. Christians also recognize that all truth is not discerned alone in the scripture, but certainly sufficient truth to guide the human venture through life. The basic faith affirmation that all truth is God's truth supports an understanding of creation as disclosing truth as well. The shared life of the Trinity extends to all dimensions of the universe. Within it there is a place for general revelation, special revelation, and the use of human reason in conjunction with experience to make sense of life. Special revelation is what Christians find in Jesus Christ and the scripture and general revelation is what is discovered in all of creation.

God's trinitarian life permeates all of creation and glimpses can be discerned to guide the thought and practice of Christian education.[7] Truth telling in teaching also calls for confronting what Sixto García identifies as "trinitarian dysfunction," or sin. This dysfunction is the failure of

4. See my discussion in Pazmiño, *God Our Teacher*, 103–11.
5. See my discussion of authority in Pazmiño, *By What Authority?*
6. G. Fackre, *Christian Story*, 17–40.
7. See Pazmiño, *God Our Teacher*, 15–36.

human persons and human structures to image the relationship of loving dialogue and shared life among the divine persons of the Trinity.[8] The truth disclosed or incarnated in loving care for persons, structures, and all of creation faithfully reflect the shared life modeled in the Trinity. The scriptural standard for this quality of individual/corporate life expressed through community is "speaking the truth in love" (Eph 4:15). Speaking includes actions as well as words and echoes God's own speaking the creation into reality (Gen 1:1–2:4; John 1:1–5). Teaching can foster the sharing of living words that issue in actions accomplishing God's purposes in the world. The re-creative possibilities of truth disclosed and discovered through teaching and learning in love holds forth a promise. The promise is of Jesus' very presence in fulfilling his commission to teach (Matt 28:18–20).

TRANSFORMATION AND RECONCILIATION

Teaching the truth in love, following the exemplary earthly ministry of Jesus, invites the transformation of persons, groups, communities, and societal structures in ways that glorify God. For this to be possible, confrontation is often required to expose the sin or dysfunction. This is the prophetic task described in the scriptures that relates to the place of challenge or stretch in teaching. The complementary movement in teaching, and more broadly in ministry, is the pastoral task of support and encouragement. The good news of God's grace and provision in the persons and ministries of Jesus Christ and the Holy Spirit complement the bad news of personal and corporate sin or dysfunction. Teaching that liberates us from sinful oppression in its diverse forms by confrontation also celebrates God's providential care and plenitude. Problem-posing teaching, of which the Brazilian educator Paulo Freire spoke, may pose conflicts that are often avoided in educational encounters.[9] Problems can be explored with an effort to find God's wisdom. The proclamation of truth through teaching involves both the denunciation of sinful patterns and the annunciation of new life God offers in Jesus Christ.

8. García, "Hispanic and Mainstream Trinitarian Theologies," 98–100; as elaborated upon in Díaz, *On Being Human*, 54–56.

9. Freire, *Pedagogy of the Oppressed*. See my discussion of Freire's thoughts in Pazmiño, *Latin American Journey*, 28–54.

The truth regarding the extent of dysfunction or sin, along with the complicity of existing structures and arrangements to support it, often cannot avoid conflict. How the conflict is resolved nonviolently requires the ministry of reconciliation of which the apostle Paul describes in 2 Corinthians 5:17—6:1:

> So if anyone is in Christ, there is a new creation: everything old has passed away; see, everything has become new! All this is from God, who reconciled us to himself through Christ, and has given us the ministry of reconciliation; that is, in Christ God was reconciling the world to himself, not counting their trespasses against them, and entrusting the message of reconciliation to us. So we are ambassadors for Christ, since God is making his appeal through us; we entreat you on behalf of Christ, be reconciled to God. For our sake he made him to be sin who knew no sin, so that in him we might become the righteousness of God. As we work together with him, we urge you also not to accept the grace of God in vain.

Trespasses and sin are directly addressed and the reconciliation is only possible once the truth is disclosed. Old patterns are transformed in the new creation made possible by God's provision of Jesus Christ. Righteousness, justice, reconciliation, and God's promised *shalom* (peace) are all possible, provided the prerequisite disclosure of the truth of our human personal and corporate condition has been shared. Daily the media provide accounts of sin and dysfunction in the world. Acceptance of God's grace also invites a continued experience of reconciliation and transformation in all dimensions of human and created life as Christians explore their public ministry.

Teaching in the name of Jesus can foster this re-creative and renewing process made available to all. But truth telling involves real risks and costs. The prophets of both the old and new covenants were not popular persons in their communities. The very suggestion of change itself can pose a conflict, given the investment in the existing status quo in many communities. Not all changes proposed fulfill God's purposes and must be seen as approximations. Spiritual discernment is required to distinguish those changes that will fulfill the righteousness, justice, peace, and *shalom* God intends for all of humanity and creation. Changes are usually balanced with points of continuity that sustain personal and communal life. Exceptions can be noted where radical transformation is the only alternative to long-standing dysfunctional patterns. This was the case in the American Revolution that resisted the oppression of England.

Accountability for the changes proposed and for sustaining renewed relationships following change requires long-standing commitments and the effort to establish trust. As related to teaching, the task is captured in the parable from Matthew 13:52: "Therefore every scribe who has been trained for the kingdom of God is like the master of a household who brings out of his treasure what is new and what is old" (NRSV).[10] Old treasures affirm points of continuity, norms, and virtues that have passed the tests of time. These old treasures can sustain persons and communities in times of transition and instability. New treasures affirm necessary points of transformation, new creations, and radical departures God is calling for us to embrace. These new treasures seek greater fulfillment of God's purposes as modeled in the life, death, and resurrection of Jesus Christ, and as empowered by the Holy Spirit in the world.

INTEGRITY

Teaching the truth in the name of Jesus also raises the crucial issue of integrity.[11] The media regularly note breaches of integrity among leaders in all areas of public and personal life. Teachers, pastors, and priests are cited for crossing boundaries in their relationships. The virtue of humility relates to truth in terms of Christians acknowledging their failings and shortcomings through confession, and by working for reconciliation in their relationships. In humility we acknowledge who we are. Some Christian traditions recognize our humble identity through receiving ashes on our foreheads to begin our Lenten journeys of self-reflection in the light of the cross.

Proclaiming the gospel through teaching requires sharing the whole counsel of God (Acts 20:27) and disclosing the beauty of God's wisdom that stands in contrast with worldly wisdom (Jas 3:13–18). Integrity is a wholeness of character modeled in Jesus. Stephen L. Carter suggests that integrity requires three steps: "(1) *discerning* what is right and what is wrong; (2) *acting* on what you have discerned, even at personal cost; and (3) *saying openly* that you are acting on your understanding of right

---

10. Conde-Frazier, *Multicultural Models*, 267.

11. See my discussion of integrity in Pazmiño, *Basics of Teaching*, 78–83.

and wrong."[12] In other words, integrity involves "the courage of our convictions, the willingness to act and speak in behalf of what we know to be right."[13] For Carter, "the first criterion captures the idea of integrity as requiring a degree of moral reflectiveness. The second criterion brings in the ideal of an integral person as steadfast, which includes the sense of keeping commitments."[14] The standard for faithfulness is God's steadfast love. Carter continues: "The third reminds us that a person of integrity is unashamed of doing the right." For Carter, a person of integrity is one "we feel we can trust to do right, to play by the rules, to keep commitments."[15] Truthfulness of the person of a teacher is at stake in terms of integrity as Carter suggests. What is incarnated in a teacher's life is a witness. James 3:1 provides a warning related to the matter of integrity of teachers: "Not many of you should become teachers, my brothers and sisters, for you know that we who teach will be judged with greater strictness." Modeling a wholeness and integrity is a life-long challenge for Christian teachers in following Jesus into their teaching settings and outside as well.

EVALUATION

The issue of integrity can be further pursued in the evaluation of teaching. Truth in one's practice of teaching calls for conscientious assessment. Given the five virtues of truth, love, faith, hope, and joy proposed for Christian teaching, evaluation can begin by exploring the following questions related to each of the virtues explored in part one. Teachers can ask themselves the following questions provided they recognize that teaching can be seen as truth through personality that honors their particular personality and calling:

1. Truth: What new and old truths did students and I discover?

2. Love: How did participants and I care for the subject(s) considered? How was I challenged to care for students in new ways and for the wider context?

3. Faith: What teaching actions or moves were effective/ineffective and why?

12. Carter, *Integrity*, 7.
13. Ibid.
14. Ibid.
15. Ibid.

4. Hope: How might I advocate for educational changes in my setting in being faithful to Jesus?

5. Joy: Identify sources of joy to celebrate in my teaching and areas to lament.

The naming of lament may pose a question, but joy can be experienced along with lament in the paradoxes of life as suggested by Habakkuk 3:17–19 where rejoicing is experienced even in the presence of loss, failure, and suffering.

TRUTH EXTENDED

Truth extended in the social, communal, and familial dimensions of life becomes wisdom that is sustained by integrity. Pope John XXIII eloquently defined wisdom as "truth that, by God's grace, moves from the mind to the heart in order to move us to live and act on it."[16] Truth needs to extend into living and acting in ways that honor the name of Jesus. More than the mind, the heart, will, and body of teacher and student alike are engaged in their encounter with truth. Only then does truth emerge as wisdom to be shared and celebrated. The movement or truth to affect all of life is dependent on God's grace for both teachers and students.

Wisdom in the scriptures is seen as a gift of God. This was the case for Solomon in 1 Kings 3 and 4, and God personifies wisdom as a virtuous woman in Proverbs 8 and 9. Proverbs describes wisdom as she is calling at the crossroads of life, sharing truth and giving instruction, modeling faithful living in the way of righteousness and justice, loving those who diligently seek, endowing wealth, filling life with joy, building a house, and setting a table for a feast. The book of 1 Corinthians notes that Jesus Christ has become our wisdom (1 Cor 1:18–25) in whom are hidden all the treasures of wisdom and knowledge (Col 2:2, 3). All of these passages affirm the divine source of wisdom.

As a teacher I continue to be amazed about what becomes lodged as wisdom in the hearts and minds of my students. They often recall what does not appear in my carefully prepared presentation notes, but make comments shared serendipitously or in response to a question posed. This recall I attribute to the gracious working of God's Spirit who extends truth to where folk are living and struggling. This wisdom finds

16. McBride, *Retreat with Pope*, 40.

expression through and, on occasion, despite me. In both cases I celebrate God's gift extended to those with whom I teach.

Truth that becomes incarnated as wisdom holds the potential of affecting one's relationships as family, community, and society. As truth is shared and is embodied in faithful living, learning is then possible. But receptivity to the truth or wisdom shared is essential. Truth discovered by personal inquiry can hold more attention than legacies passed along, especially when change affects both persons and their contexts. Changing times call for the revisiting of truths proclaimed in relation to perennial questions. These truths may well be reaffirmed, but each generation is invited through teaching and learning to discern wisdom. The process of discerning wisdom is shared within the Christian community. It requires that we ask God for gifts of wisdom hidden in Jesus Christ. The wisdom of poet and essayist James Russell Lowell is worth citing. Lowell noted that "New occasions teach new duties, time makes ancient good uncouth. They must upward still and onward, who would keep abreast of truth."[17] Keeping abreast of truth is a life long calling for Christian teachers and students.

Truth as emphasized in this chapter can become a hard reality if not balanced and wed with love, and that is the focus of chapter three. Nevertheless, love without the truth can become soft in not providing the disclosure of reality called for in life that can occasion God's wisdom and transformation. The apostle Paul reminds us in 1 Corinthians 13:6 that love "rejoices in the truth."

17. Lowell as cited in Bosch, *Transforming Mission*, 47.

3

Love and Teaching in the Name of Jesus

ONE LOVING SPIRIT

A QUOTE THAT HAS always fascinated me regarding teaching comes from the great African teacher of the Christian Church, Augustine of Hippo. Augustine observed that "one loving spirit sets another spirit on fire."[1] Exploring love in relation to teaching in the name of Jesus provides a variety of perspectives to consider.

First, there is the love itself that undergirds and anchors all Christian teaching. That love takes on a particular quality when its generative source traces back to Jesus of Nazareth and his earthly life, ministry, and example. First John 4:10 makes explicit the source: "In this is love, no that we loved God but that he loved us and sent his Son to be the atoning sacrifice for our sins." Henri Nouwen elaborates on the implications of this scriptural insight for Christian teachers:

> The great message that we have to carry, as ministers of God's word
> and followers of Jesus, is that God loves us not because of what we
> do or accomplish, but because God has created and redeemed us
> in love and has chosen us to proclaim that love as the true source
> of all human life.[2]

For Christians, Jesus is the exemplary teacher who sets the model for all persons following him as disciples.[3] Jesus is the model for loving, as well as our primary source for understanding both the love of God and the highest expressions of human love. The new commandment Jesus proposes for his disciples is found in John 13:34–35: "I give you a new

---

1. Augustine of Hippo, *Confessions*, Book IV, chapter 14, paragraph 21.

2. Nouwen, *Name of Jesus*, 17.

3. See my discussion of Jesus as teacher in Pazmiño, *God Our Teacher*, 59–86.

commandment that you love one another. Just as I have loved you, you also should love one another. By this everyone will know that you are my disciples, if you have love for one another." Jesus demonstrated his love for humanity and all of creation through his life, death on a cross, and resurrection. This love does not exclude an exploration of the truth as explored in chapter two. Jesus' love extends to being an advocate for Christians today through his intercession (1 John 2:1) and sending the Holy Spirit who also intercedes for Christians (John 14:26; 15:26; 16:7; Rom 8:26). Teaching and the love of teaching manifested in everyday teaching acts become a visible expression of one's love for others. Following in the tradition of Jesus provides hints for how current-day teachers can express their love for teaching by sharing their lives as well as their teaching. The apostle Paul suggests that this provides one standard for Christian teachers, namely sharing their lives as well as the gospel (1 Thess 2:8; 1 Tim 4:16).

Second, the calling to teach in the particular name of Jesus itself generates a human love in response to the gracious divine love made most explicit in the life, death, resurrection, and ascension of God's Son. Jesus taught his disciples as with friends, brothers, and sisters (John 15:15; Matt 12:46–50). First John 4:19 makes explicit this love connection with God made manifest in Jesus: "We love because he first loved us." If as teachers we experience a deficit of love with our students, we need to explore in greater depth God's love for us as God's beloved. The experience of God's love in Christ also issues in a commandment: "The commandment we have from him is this: those who love God must love their brothers and sisters also" (1 John 4:21). Teaching is one vehicle for expressing our direct love for God through interaction with actual or potential brothers and sisters in the Christian faith. Love of neighbor becomes an obligation, an expected response, for teachers as recipients of God's great love. Loving God whom we do not see is incarnated through diverse ministries of teaching with folk whom we do see: "Those who say 'I love God,' and hate their brothers or sisters are liars; for those who do not love a brother or sister whom they have seen, cannot love God whom they have not seen" (1 John 4:20). This is also in some sense the lessons of Matthew 25 regarding the nations applied to teaching with the piercing words of Jesus: "Truly I tell you, just as you did it to one of the least of these who are members of my family, you did it to me" (Matt 25:40). What do our corporate commitments to teaching the least of Jesus' family reveal about our love for God? God's love initiates and calls forth a response that can be channeled through faithful teaching.

Third, as suggested by Augustine's quote, the gracious movement of the Holy Spirit in human hearts as evidenced in Jesus' life now activates a loving spirit in human hearts. Romans 5:6 supports this insight: "Hope does not disappoint us, because God's love has been poured into our hearts through the Holy Spirit that has been given to us." The presence of the Holy Spirit activates human teaching abilities with a love that transforms them. Teaching becomes a spiritual gift by which the love of God is experienced through the caring and confronting actions of teachers. The loving spirit of the teacher as anointed by the Holy Spirit sets the spirits of students on fire to become all God intends for them. The Spirit empowers the efforts of teachers to both support and challenge students fulfilling the two great commandments of Jesus to love God with all of our heart, soul, mind, and strength, and our neighbors as ourselves (Luke 10:27). Beyond the example and responsive obligation of love, comes the empowerment to love through the person and ministry of God's Spirit who enables us to care.

CARE

Our love of teaching in the name of Jesus is one measure of our care quotient and the stewardship of our lives. How do we care for the content, persons, and context of our various teaching ministries? Education itself can be defined as the process of sharing content with persons in the context of their community and society. Care needs to be exercised in the three teaching phases of preparation, instruction, and evaluation.[4] The time and energy invested in careful preparation for teaching can serve as spiritual offerings in service to God and others. Committing to God any teaching plans that are developed in prayer can foster an openness and flexibility. Prayer for all the participants in a teaching event can serve as accessing spiritual wells to transform the experience. Prayer serves to honor the essential role of God as teacher in all of life, and to foster active listening on the part of teachers. Prayer is not limited to the preparation phase of teaching. Silent prayer during the actual instruction itself provides perspective in responding to issues and inquiries that unexpectedly

4. See my discussion of care in relation to teaching in Pazmiño, *Basics of Teaching*, and especially in relationship to love, 83–88.

surface. Even during evaluation after actual instruction, prayer has helped to discern the need for follow-up with particular persons. As such this prayer has helped the transfer of learning outside the teaching event. It has also confirmed the need for new directions in subsequent teaching encounters. The prayer for participants prior to, during, and after teaching thus serves as one measure of the care teachers can exercise. This prayerful care is one expression of love following the example and tradition of Jesus and, thereby, teaching in his name.

PERSONS TO LOVE

In returning to the elements of content, persons, and context in teaching, other thoughts emerge. Persons are of infinite worth and dignity being created in the image of God. Teachers express their love by honoring the potential of each and every person as a child of God, a sister or brother of Jesus Christ, and a vessel of the Holy Spirit with unique gifts. Teaching is to draw out and provide support for the discovery, sharing, and development of persons' gifts for a wide variety of callings. Even the most resistant and uncooperative participant in a teaching encounter represents a person needing to experience some dimension of God's care. On some occasions care comes in the form of confronting persons with their irresponsibility and wider accountability. My general tactic is to confront issues of discipline in private, but on occasion I have proposed a group response to destructive behaviors. This, of course, applies to my need as a teacher to ask for forgiveness for my own behavior and words when unnecessary offense has resulted. Love involves a willingness to address dysfunctional personal and corporate patterns and structures. The presence of sin impacts the teaching setting and calls for a faithful response in the light of the gospel of Jesus Christ.[5] God's love and grace transcend the impacts of sin and dysfunction in teaching and all the activities of created and creative life.

Jesus' interaction with Peter recorded in John 21:15–19 offers an example of how the love of persons applies to the nurture possible in Christian teaching. Peter's love of Jesus failed in his denial prior to the crucifixion, but after the resurrection Jesus reinstates Peter and exhorts him to express his love through his ministry with others:

---

5. I discuss the impact of sin in Pazmiño, *God Our Teacher*, 37–57.

Love and Teaching in the Name of Jesus

When they had finished breakfast, Jesus said to Simon Peter, "Simon son of John, do you love more than these?" He said to him, "Yes, Lord; you know that I love you." Jesus said to him, "Feed my lambs." A second time he said to him, "Simon son of John, do you love me?" He said to him, "Yes, Lord; you know that I love you." Jesus said to him, "Tend my sheep." He said to him the third time, "Simon son of John, do you love me?" Peter felt hurt because he said to him the third time, "Do you love me?" And he said to him, "Lord, you know everything; you know that I love you." Jesus said to him, "Feed my sheep. Very truly, I tell you, when you were younger, you used to fasten your own belt and to go wherever you wished. But when you grow old, you will stretch out your hands, and someone else will fasten a belt around you and take you where you do not wish to go." (He said this to indicate the kind of death by which he would glorify God.) After this he said to him, "Follow me."

Peter's love of Jesus was to find expression in his feeding others, as Christian teaching intends to accomplish. The threefold commission to feed or tend sheep and lambs involves the shepherding ministry of teaching. Christian teaching requires a sustained and abiding love of Jesus and persons. This love contrasts with Peter's performance in relation to Jesus prior to and at the crucifixion. Nevertheless, Jesus' grace following the resurrection reinstates Peter and solidifies his commitment of love to Jesus. Peter then channels this love into his ministry. This action implies, to me, the care and teaching of those he is called to serve.

THE LOVE OF TEACHING

Fostering the love of teaching is a lifelong task, an art and craft that is nurtured in dialogue with others. The search for a quick fix, or the one ideal teaching method or approach to resolving the various challenges and paradoxes of teaching, is a futile effort. Careful attention to a variety of factors impacting the content, persons, and context of any teaching will develop with experience and critical reflection over time. One dimension of that journey involves the exercise of self-care. With the increasing numbers of hurting persons in society and teaching settings, the wisdom shared by my colleague Kirk Jones in his book *Rest in the Storm* provides a necessary perspective. Jones suggests that "We do our best work when we are rooted in who we are."[6] All that we are as persons reflects God's loving

6. K. Jones, *Rest in the Storm*, 48.

gifts at birth and throughout our lives (Jas 1:17–18). For the Christian teacher that rootedness is based upon our identity as children of God, disciples of Jesus Christ, and vessels of the Holy Spirit. A prayer of Augustine of Hippo, a great teacher of the church, serves as a reminder of the Spirit's ministry with teachers:

> Breathe in me O Holy Spirit, that my thoughts may all be holy; Act in me O Holy Spirit, that my work, too, may be holy; Draw my heart O Holy Spirit, that I love but what is holy; Strengthen me O Holy Spirit, to defend all that is holy; Guard me, then, O Holy Spirit, that I always may be holy. Amen.[7]

The teacher's partnership with the Holy Spirit, sustained through prayer, first provides a life-sustaining root for teaching ministries with hurting folk. Second, the various crises that impact local, national, and global contexts call for a loving and discerning response sustained by spiritual resources. Third, the vast proliferation of information and knowledge contending for attention in the content of teaching require a wisdom God's Spirit promises to those who ask (Jas 1:5–7; Eph 1:17).

A WELL-SET TABLE

The love of teaching in Jesus' name also has implications for the wider context of all the historical, social, cultural, political, financial, sexual, intellectual, ideological, and spiritual relations that characterize human and created life. Teachers need to attend to these realities if persons are to become all God intends for them. Honoring the voices of those marginalized and oppressed, known as the *anawim*, is essential to welcome all to the metaphorical table of teaching. No persons are to remain under the table and excluded from the feast shared at the invitation of Jesus. As the gift of loaves and fishes is prayed over with thanksgiving and is multiplied with twelve baskets leftover in feeding hungry persons (Matt 12:13–21; Mark 6:30–44; Luke 9:10–17; John 6:1–14), so Christian teachers need to advocate for full access to the teaching resources available to them. The Christian teacher is called to be attentive to those on the margins and to ministry in all areas of life, thereby extending God's love in Christ.

---

7. Augustine, "Prayer for the Indwelling."

LOVE EXTENDED

Love extended in the social, communal, and familial dimensions of life becomes a commitment to peace and justice in all of God's creation. All of creation hungers for the promise of God's shalom that ultimately fulfills God's love for the world. "God so loved the world that He gave his only Son" (John 3:16), and that world awaits the fulfillment of eternal life as God intended it from creation. What is it that Christian teachers can give as expressions of their social and communal love?

Elizabeth Conde-Frazier describes a spiritual journey toward peaceful living from hospitality to shalom.[8] That journey requires a sustained commitment to building peace through justice as values God holds for humanity. Because all persons are created in God's image they are deserving of care and respect. Creation itself is God's legacy that requires stewardship and care. With all that divides humanity, Christian teachers are to be about ministries of reconciliation, and building peace where enmity, strife, and conflict have prevailed. Initially, as Conde-Frazier outlines, teaching ministries begin with hospitality and encounter demonstrating compassion and passion with the ultimate goal of shalom.[9] This journey calls for love of one's neighbor who may be radically different from oneself, but the extent of such love is exemplified for Christian teachers in Jesus.

CRUCIFORM LOVE

The extent of God's love incarnated in Jesus' life and ministry is demonstrated in his death upon the cross. In chapter one the theological touchstone of the crucifixion is noted. For Christian teachers the practical question is how to demonstrate the distinguishing virtue of agape love through their ministries. From my twenty-seven years of teaching experience I cannot propose an easy formula to follow. This is the case because each particular context for teaching, and the variety of persons gathered for their learning, represents a distinctive invitation to engage other persons. In an earlier work that explores the basics of teaching I suggested that love is demonstrated in the careful attention given to preparation, instruction, and evaluation.[10] Beyond these basics I would add the

8. Conde-Frazier, "Spiritual Journey," 158–85.

9. Ibid.

10. Pazmiño, *Basics of Teaching*.

additional virtue of humility. This virtue calls teachers to recognize the limits of our human love and the need to be dependent upon God's resources to complement our capabilities. Christian teachers are partners with the Holy Spirit to attend to truth and to encourage a faithful response by persons, communities, and the wider society to God's demands. Love requires that first those demands weigh heavy upon the lives of teachers: "A disciple is not above the teacher, but everyone who is fully qualified will be like the teacher" (Luke 6:40).

The willingness of the teacher to be a model or mentor assumes a vulnerability and availability that can often be at a premium in a time-pressed culture and lifestyle. Excellence in teaching as in all areas of ministry is costly in terms of the commitment, time, and energies of those called. Such cruciform love in the teaching practices requires both attention to the details of student learning and a willingness to develop a craft and art form over time. Teachers are also called to have a teachable spirit in honoring their continual learning and sharing with passion what they themselves and other persons are discovering together.

Beyond the subject matters or content of any teaching encounter, Christian teachers are called to have an interest in the persons of their students. Sharing an interest in the life journeys of students and their extended relationships outside of the classroom holds the potential of relating the teaching content to life. Teaching, while obviously public, needs to be vulnerable enough to consider an engagement with public issues. To do this responsibly requires a freedom for students to disagree with any position of advocacy that a teacher may assume on issues of the day. One of those issues includes the question of educational equity with deference of various forms operating in the wider culture of human societies. Jesus' encounter with the Samaritan woman in John highlights this issue as explored in chapter nine.

EDUCATIONAL EQUITY

In terms of multicultural education for current teaching practice, that full access implies educational equity. Educational equity can be defined in terms of access to educational resources, respect of difference, space to be heard, the presence of appropriate role models, and shared power and authority at all levels of educational programs in representative proportion.[11] Such a definition of equity is an ideal that calls for the expression of love in the social sphere of our lives. Love in the social sphere embodies justice along with a concern for righteousness in all human relationships. Loving persons in the public and social sphere requires addressing those conditions that prevent a just and equitable life for all of God's children. Love involves caring enough to confront patterns of exclusion and injustice that historically have plagued educational institutions and structures. The impacts of racism, sexism, classism, and other forms of oppression have ravaged the educational opportunities and experiences of far too many persons and groups. The loving response to these realities calls for seeing that one of the tasks of teaching is to confront the destroyers of life. These destroyers are manifest in different forms that call for spiritual engagement to make a concrete difference for the "common good" (1 Cor 12:7). Teachers are called to love and care enough to speak up and act. As a teacher I will remember the comments of one student who noted on a course evaluation, "I sensed you loved us in this course." I am sure there was contrary evidence for some students suggesting otherwise in that course. Teachers may hope for similar comments to that of my grandson Oliver, as noted in the introduction, who softly told his mother that he loved Mindi his teacher. But Christian teachers can hope that the love of students eventually transfers to their love of God. After his resurrection, Jesus three times posed a question to Peter that is posed for us who teach in his name: "Do you love me?" (John 21:15–19). In response to Peter's affirmation of love, Jesus commanded him to feed his lambs, tend his sheep, and feed his sheep. Teaching is one ministry in which to express our love for Jesus.

The promise of transformative teaching that loves in our deeds, as well as our words, follows in the steps of Jesus of Nazareth and gives honor to his name. Christians or "Christ-bearers" bear the wonderful name of Jesus and are called to honor that name in their living and teaching. Those who followed Jesus were first referred to as Christians in the multicultural church setting of Antioch (Acts 11:26), and yet the multicultural character of that particular church is too often ignored. Honoring Jesus' name calls for the exercise of faith, the next virtue to be considered in relation to teaching.

---

11. Pazmiño, *Latin American Journey*, 84 and 117.

4

Faith and Teaching in the Name of Jesus

FAITH IN BEING SENT

TEACHING IN JESUS' NAME is directly related to faith. Faith finds expression in the active engagement of mission. Craig Dykstra, in his recent work *Growing in the Life of Faith*, includes a brief chapter on "Learning to Be Sent." God's calling persons includes the central mission of being sent. Dykstra makes two striking claims about Christian teaching: "First, all Christian nurture and education are for the sake of mission. That's why we do it. That's its purpose. Second, nurture and education are themselves forms of mission."[1] He further suggests that "Christian education is the mission of sending people into mission and going with them."[2] I want to suggest that faith undergirds the mission of being sent and the prior teaching mission of preparing folk to go. Faith is required to discern the nature of God's calling and our human response of mission and vocation. Dykstra points out that we are sent "by Christ into whatever betrays God's purpose and love—wherever that might be. And we are sent not to bring a message of our own but to be the sent people of God there, to be signs of the presence of God there."[3] This is a comprehensive vision to embrace in teaching, but it is one that nurtures faith, and in so doing, represents the name of Jesus. Nurture itself and teaching are forms of Christian mission in the world.

Being sent, and on occasion sent out from one's home community and culture, is a faith venture. Being sent calls for trust in the actual mission and the resources required to complete the mission. For Christians,

1. Dykstra, *Growing in the Faith*, 159.
2. Ibid., 161.
3. Ibid., 159.

the identity and authority of the one sending or commissioning the effort is key. While teaching in New England for the past twenty-seven years I have often introduced myself as a missionary from Brooklyn, New York. A countercultural stance is involved if I further identify myself as a New York Yankee fan in rival Boston Red Sox territory. This introduction has often resulted in a number of laughs from participants in a public gathering and also requires definite faith in the hospitality of the group, even if baseball loyalties are raised. In actuality I was raised as an anti-Yankee fan from my native Brooklyn, but accommodated my commitments by marrying into a strongly affiliated Yankee clan that now includes my daughter. My brother and son ironically are strong Red Sox fans. Why all this association with baseball affiliations? My identity as a follower of Jesus Christ requires a missionary status even if I was ministering in my native New York City among Yankee fans. The matter of one's loyalties and commitments is crucial in the issues and actions of one's life, well beyond the national pastime of baseball. Being sent and equipped by God fosters the taking of risks, beyond disclosing baseball matters, to include those of life and death. The venture of Christian teaching calls for faith in one's own identity as a teacher and the presence of God's Spirit to empower the effort.

A CALL FOR ACTION

Teaching calls for action in being sent that includes preparation, instruction, and evaluation with persons who can learn.[4] The New Testament book of James closely associates faith with actions or works (Jas 1:19–27; 2:14–26), and faith manifests itself in works. In teaching, these works include the tasks of thinking, reflecting, organizing, greeting, speaking, listening, responding, questioning, disciplining, and affirming. Thomas F. Green, in his expansive work *The Activities of Teaching*, analyzes teaching into logical acts and strategic acts. The logical acts include explaining, concluding, inferring, giving reasons, amassing evidence, demonstrating, defining, and comparing. The strategic acts include motivating, counseling, evaluating, planning, encouraging, disciplining, and questioning. He also describes the institutional acts in school settings of collecting money, chaperoning, patrolling halls, attending meetings, taking attendance,

---

4. I analyze the basics of teaching this way in Pazmiño, *Basics of Teaching*.

consulting parents, and keeping reports.[5] Each of those tasks or activities can embody a faithful or effective expression of God's care and concern for persons in a public or religious setting.

Honoring God's care also requires receptivity to what participants offer in the teaching event. From my recent return to an occasional teaching with preschool children, after years of primarily working with adult learners, I was amazed with the variety of the children's responses. But what transcended the activities was a hunger for relationships and the sharing facilitated over a time of snacks at a common table. My sharing the joy of becoming a grandfather for the first time fostered a reflective moment when a number of the children shared their experiences with babies, as well as what it was like to be growing up now with their own bigger hands and feet. A sense of wonder was shared over juice and cookies that ministered to all, and captured for me how the virtue of faith finds expression in Christian teaching.

A FAITH-LIFE CONNECTION

Faith can issue in actions not only in the lives of teachers, but also in the lives of students or participants. Dykstra's emphasis on "learning to be sent" encourages the inclusion of actual responses that transfer outside the teaching setting. Faith is intended to be experiential. The faith-life connection in Christian teaching ushers in faithful life practices.[6] Working with preschoolers and their levels of activity and shorter attention spans poses the challenge of what students retain upon leaving their Sunday school classes. More than take-home papers and craft projects, teachers wonder what difference might be possible from their efforts. This becomes a matter for prayer along with careful preparation for each session. Such wonder with children extends to settings with youth and adults. In addition, the matter of modeling is one that applies to the experiences in the classroom, the home, and the wider faith community.

Children learn much from imitation, and time spent together with faithful and caring adults over time can make a difference from my life experience. I recall those teachers who shared their lives by

---

5. Green, *Activities of Teaching*, 4. Green's analysis applies the insights of linguistic analysis to teaching that can include Christian as well as public settings.

6. Dean and Foster provide a helpful list and discussion of Christian practices in their work *Godbearing Life*, 105–22.

remembering my birthday with a cake or laughing at my skill in finding the shortest scripture verses like John 11:35 and 1 Thessalonians 5:16 and 17 for Bible memory assignments. These experiences are transformative, but are complemented with times for reflection. Those loving actions of teachers were associated with God's love and their vibrant and living Christian faith. Teaching calls for informed or examined experience to avoid a neo-romanticism in overemphasizing human potentials limited by our sin. Discipline is required to guide the experiences of preschoolers and all ages of students in Christian teaching. Faith is tested and tried with the harsh realities of life and the presence of sin in personal and corporate life. Personal faith and experience need communal examination and confirmation along with the correctives of the Christian tradition that itself is reformed over time.

DIMENSIONS OF FAITH

The exercise of faith in teaching can be seen in relation to a traditional theological understanding of faith itself. Faith can be viewed in terms of the dimensions of *notitia* (intellectual affirmation), *assensus* (affective affirmation), and *fiducia* (intentional affirmation). The additional dimension could be behavioral, building upon the activities or practices that Green proposed for teaching. Christian teaching can expand upon Green's listing to include the specific activities of prayer, meditation, scripture reading, and other spiritual practices that can both undergird and be directly performed during instruction. One student in a recent teaching course learned of the practice of prayer preparation prior to teaching and even silently praying for participants during instruction that I noted was possible. She faithfully participates in prayer, but never made the direct connection to her teaching practice, until it was specifically noted and actually practiced in the classroom as graduate students disclosed specific prayer needs in their lives.

In relation to the intellectual dimension of faith, teachers are called to bring every thought captive to the mind of Christ, as suggested by 2 Corinthians 10:4b–5: "We destroy arguments and every proud obstacle raised up against the knowledge of God, and we take every thought captive to obey Christ." Having the mind of Christ calls for imitating his humility as the Philippians 2:5–8 passage teaches:

43

> Let the same mind be in you that was in Christ Jesus, who, though
> he was in the form of God, did not regard equality with God as
> something to be exploited, but emptied himself, taking the form of
> a slave, being born in human likeness. And being found in human
> form, he humbled himself and became obedient to the point of
> death—even death on a cross.

There is no place for intellectual pride in teaching, but rather in seeking to love God with all of one's mind reflecting the glories of God's creation and divine wisdom that stands in contrast with human wisdom (Jas 3:13–18).

The affective dimension of faith finds expression in teaching through the heartfelt affirmation of God's revelation of care and lament in relation to God's creation and humanity's plight. Because God cares for persons and the restoration of fellowship made possible in Jesus Christ through the ministry of the Holy Spirit, teachers extend that care in their relationships with students, the wider community, and society. The expression of lamentation is appropriate in the light of human suffering that includes all of creation that groans until God's promised consummation is experienced:

> We know that the whole creation has been groaning in labor pains
> until now; and not only the creation, but we ourselves, who have
> been the first fruits of the Spirit, groan inwardly while we wait for
> adoption, the redemption of our bodies. (Rom 8:22–23)

The expression of our feelings relates to loving God with all of our heart and soul that is attended to in the affective dimension of teaching (Luke 10:27).[7]

The intentional dimension of teaching for me relates to the matter of commitment, devotion, and discipline. One exemplary model for devotion is found in Ezra, the scribe God used to provide leadership during a time of struggle and transition in the life of Israel. As noted in Ezra 7:10: "Ezra had set his heart to study the law of the Lord, and to do it, and to teach that statutes and ordinances in Israel." The setting of the heart speaks of devotion, dedication, and commitment even at personal cost to Ezra. The matter of devotion and commitment is a major challenge in an age that glorifies personal comfort and pleasure. Faithful service

---

7. See Moore, *Teaching from the Heart*, ix, who addresses the quality of teaching in referring to the heart in receiving and giving the Spirit of Life.

can be demanding and costly, and too often avoided with a preference for the quick fix in all areas of life. The model of Jesus' life, especially in terms of the cross, poses a distinct alternative to many cultural norms and preferred practices in both personal and corporate life. The noteworthy exception to this pattern is what women in many settings have been expected to fulfill in caring for others. Carol Lakey Hess exposes this pattern in *Caretakers of Our Common House* where self-sacrifice becomes a sin at the expense of the self-development of women.[8] Christian teachers of both genders need to be caretakers of our own house (self) as well as our common house (faith community and world). In this effort our intentions and commitments need to be as clear as possible. We also need corrective and constructive evaluation from those who know and love us well. The alternative is unfaithful stewardship of our teaching gifts and callings. Surrendering to the risks and accepting the costs of teaching requires us, in some ways, to decrease so that Christ may increase. Abiding in Christ calls us to take up the cross daily and to identify with the suffering of others who become our neighbors in the light of Jesus' cross (Luke 9:23). We exercise faith in trusting God for the results of our efforts and the faithfulness of others to what they have learned with us.

FAITH EXTENDED

Faith extended in the social, communal, and familial dimensions of life becomes discipleship and citizenship in mission. Discipleship and citizenship are expressions of Christian service. These are the works of faith about which the book of James emphasizes (Jas 1:19–27; 2:14–26). Christian teaching attends to the formation of disciples of Jesus and citizens of God's creation.[9] The challenges of both discipleship and citizenship vary with the context and calling of each follower of Jesus. Teachers pose questions for students in terms of how their faith extends into the places of their whole lives. Faith practices, such as scripture reading and prayer, serve to provide ritual containers for discerning the contours of what following Jesus means each day. These rituals also discern what new ventures need to be launched personally and corporately in response to the gospel. Dialogue with other Christians globally is crucial in the process

8. Hess, *Caretakers of our Common House*, 38.

9. On these themes see Boys, *Education for Citizenship*; and J. Jones, *Traveling Together*.

of discernment. Dialogue is also crucial over the centuries with Christians of past eras and with one's faith community's particular history and traditions. The faith connections to teaching are deepened in this effort.

FAITH CONNECTION TO TEACHING

The faith connection to teaching and education has been discussed by a number of Christian educators beyond my thoughts here. For example, Mary C. Boys in *Educating in Faith*, explored various maps and visions regarding the task of teaching in faith communities.[10] Richard Osmer wrote *Teaching For Faith* with a focus upon adult learners and teaching for belief, relationship, commitment, and mystery.[11] Thomas H. Groome wrote *Sharing Faith* with a stress upon conation or wisdom in relation to his shared praxis approach.[12] It is noteworthy that when Harold Burgess reflected upon the entire field of religious education in 1996, he cited Boys, Osmer, and Groome as contemporary writers of significance along with Timothy Lines.[13] The faith of teaching in the name of Jesus calls for reflection as shared in writings and actions incarnated in practices that give glory to that name. This is the scriptural standard set in Colossians 3:17: "And whatever you do, in word or deed, do everything in the name of the Lord Jesus, giving thanks to God the Father through him." The giving of thanks flows from the recognition that faith itself is a gift of God that calls for our holistic life response and faithful actions. That response includes the affirmation of hope, which is the virtue for focus of chapter five.

10. Boys, *Educating in Faith*.
11. Osmer, *Teaching For Faith*.
12. Groome, *Sharing Faith*.
13. Burgess, *Models of Religious Education*, 226–33.

5

Hope and Teaching in the Name of Jesus

HOPE'S DAUGHTERS: ANGER AND COURAGE

TEACHING INVOLVES A NUMBER of risks and factors that call for consideration in the preparation, instruction, and evaluation phases of teaching.[1] Christian teachers are called to rest in God's gracious working despite, through, and beyond us in our partnership with the Holy Spirit. The great teacher of the Christian Church Augustine of Hippo observed that "Hope has two lovely daughters, anger and courage. Anger at the way things are, and courage to see that they need not remain as they are."[2] Besides Jesus and Paul, Augustine stands as a highly influential Christian teacher over the centuries.[3]

This quote from Augustine has impacted my thoughts on teaching because I too have two lovely daughters, one by birth and one by marriage. Rebekah, now age twenty-five, is my daughter by birth. After majoring in sociology and Latino studies, she is currently a law student who advocates for the needs of those marginalized. She works in the area of public advocacy and capital defense. Larisa is my daughter by marriage. She is a development officer and grant writer for Facing History and Ourselves, an international educational and professional organization whose mission is to help students from diverse backgrounds to consider the affects of racism, prejudice, and anti-Semitism. The organization's purpose is to promote the development of a more humane and informed citizenry.

1. I discuss these phases in Pazmiño, *Basics of Teaching*.
2. As cited in McKeachie, *Teaching Tips*, 384. This work is a helpful practical guide for teaching.
3. Augustine, while being influential, can be critiqued for separating the body and soul in his teaching and for his distorted view of women evident in his writings.

Larisa is also the mother of my first grandchild, Oliver Albert Pazmiño. When I think of my daughters' lives and vocational commitments, I think of hope for the future where the needs of others leads to lives of service and advocacy in the wider public community. How is it possible for teaching to foster hope for youth and young adults in their life choices and vocations? The expression of rage in the life of local communities and the wider society is related to a sense of hopelessness that many are experiencing in their personal lives and as they look at the state of the world around them.

Teaching in the name of Jesus can offer an alternative and foster a sense of hope for persons, families, groups, and communities. The apostle Paul, in his letter to the Ephesians, described the experiences of persons before coming to faith in Jesus Christ as "having no hope and without God in the world" (Eph 2:12). In his influential work *Race Matters*, Cornel West advocates for a politics of conversion that provides "a chance for people to believe there is hope for the future and a meaning to struggle" that Christian faith provides.[4] His politics apply to African Americans and all folk who hunger for freedom, liberation, and a new life. Those on the margins of society, those I identify as the *anawim*, particularly hunger for an alternative life.[5] It was the *anawim* to whom Jesus paid particular attention in his teaching ministry. As Christian teachers we can ask ourselves: Who are those who feel life is hopeless? How are Christians making a difference with those persons?

THE *ANAWIM*

The *anawim* are those who are poor, humble, or weak before God and others. They often represent outsiders in communities. By virtue of our created nature, sin, and suffering, all persons may see themselves at some point in their lives as one of the *anawim*. But some folk experience this status on a persistent daily basis because of the forces of racism, sexism, classism, ageism, and a host of oppressions. In relation to the wider societal and structural forces of oppression, Christian teachers are called to engage a spiritual warfare that rebukes principalities and powers in the name of Jesus (Eph 6:10–20). The very name of Jesus suggests hope because of

4. West, *Race Matters*, 18.

5. See my discussion of the *anawim* in Pazmiño, *By What Authority?*, 63–65, 69, 77, 99, and 144.

the conversion or transformation that is offered in him. This transformation impacts the personal, familial, communal, cultural, economic, social, political, intellectual, and spiritual dimensions of life. Jesus and his teaching impact all of life. In other words, transformation is possible in all of life despite the suffering, loss, and sin that plagues the human condition. This is a message of hope to share broadly and widely with all persons in one's teaching in Jesus' name. Jesus' words suggest the urgency of sharing: "Those who are ashamed of me and of my words, of them the Son of Man will be ashamed when he comes in his glory and the glory of the Father and of the holy angels" (Luke 9:26). Honoring the name of Jesus requires sharing the basis for our Christian hope. Hope in God does not shame or disappoint us because of God's integrity, reliability, love, and faithfulness to promises. This message the apostle Paul celebrates in Romans 5:5: "and hope does not disappoint us, because God's love has been poured into our hearts through the Holy Spirit that has been given to us." Hope offered in the name of Jesus provides alternatives for the *anawim* and all those persons who recognize their daily need for new life and transformation. *Anawim* are folk most in need of the hope Jesus offers.

ADVOCACY

Affirming the place of advocacy in teaching is a hopeful venture. Advocacy involves confronting and countering the destroyers of life, as well as giving voice to those who have been silenced. This stance is taken in the light of God's purposes finding expression in the world. The vision of *shalom* that God discloses in the scriptures embodies peace and a fullness of life for all of creation. In the coming of Jesus, God's reign has been initiated while waiting future fulfillment that the scriptures describe as "the already" and "not yet" of God's kingdom and "kin-dom."[6] This "kin-dom" affirms all persons becoming as adopted kin in God's family that includes "the other" as neighbor and all believers as children of God. The *anawim* are welcome at the table of God's setting where righteousness and justice are matters for discussion. The table talk excludes no one who previously may have been assigned to remain under the table. Advocacy demands that all be welcome as full guests with equitable access to the resources that are graciously and lavishly served by God and sufficient

---

6. See Isasi-Díaz, *Mujerista Theology*, 103, n. 8, for discussion of the "kin-dom" as preferred to kingdom that suggests gender and familial inclusion.

for all (Prov 9:1–6; Isa 55:1–3a). Teaching using this metaphor is putting the feast on the table so that all may participate and joyously celebrate God's plentitude and graceful bounty in life. God's table fellowship, which began at creation, was extended at the incarnation and set again prior to the crucifixion at the Lord's Supper. The Christians' table is Jesus' and it extends from the Passover table set on Holy or Maundy Thursday to the final marriage supper described in the book of Revelation 19:7–9.[7] The table is open to the participation of all as suggested by Jesus' parable of the wedding banquet (Matt 22:1–14). However, the matter of attire is raised. For me this attire metaphorically suggests the guests' acceptance of God's provision made available in Jesus Christ for salvation. This recognizes the freedom of guests to come and, when at the table, to accept or reject God's gracious offer of transformation in the name of Jesus. In the actual practice of teaching from a stance of advocacy, teachers need the balance of inquiry and dialogue to allow participants the freedom to disagree.

TIME PERSPECTIVES

A discussion of hope in relation to teaching raises the issue of time perspective. The teacher Augustine wrote of "the present of things past, the present of things present, and the present of things in the future."[8] Whereas hope focuses on the present of things future, perspective is only provided in considering both the past and present in relation to the future. Anticipation for the future is built upon memory of the past and current-day attention in the present. Teaching can provide the reflective space and time to consider the future in connection with the all-too-forgotten past. The past provides a source for identity and tradition. In relation to the past, students can explore points of continuity and change. Christian tradition honors the place of history and affirms God who enters time and space in the form of a person, Jesus of Nazareth. Christian faith celebrates God who is alive and active in current and everyday human affairs. Christian hope affirms a God who is leading creation toward a longed-for consummation yet to be revealed in Jesus Christ, but with glimpses of fulfillment in his earthly ministry. These glimpses find fruition in the continuing ministry of the Holy Spirit to bring renewal and

---

7. Debra Dean Murphy sees the table fellowship of the Eucharist as "an act of resistance that forms and transforms those who worship," in *Teaching that Transforms*, 106.

8. Augustine, *Augustine's Confessions*, 114.

transformation. Human suffering, fragmentation, and meaninglessness are not the final words because of the living hope found in the gospel of Jesus Christ (1 Pet 1:3–12). A two-week visit to China in 2000 convinced me again of this living hope as evidenced in the lives of Chinese Christians. They were sustained through the trials of the Cultural Revolution as their churches and seminaries have now reopened or been newly built to accommodate increasing numbers of youth and young adults with their spiritual hunger and calling. This hunger is being satisfied in the gospel of Jesus Christ and his calling to new life.

JESUS OUR EXEMPLAR

The hope of teaching in Jesus' name extends to his exemplary model of discipling and developing people to become all that God intends for them to be and become over time. The incarnation itself embodies God's intentions and purposes for humankind in the life and ministry of Jesus. God, though transcendent, has not been distanced from the human dilemma. By taking on human flesh Jesus identifies with all persons, and models a sustaining, risk-taking, and transforming love. The risks included death upon a cross, followed by a longed-for resurrection to a new life lived in the spirit. The promised Spirit arrived at Pentecost to offer power and authority to extend the ministry of Jesus globally (Acts 1–2). Peter and John follow Jesus' example in their Spirit-empowered teaching ministries described in Acts 2 through 5. In addition, Jesus' teaching ministry over time has extended the range of his earthly ministry to include followers in many corners of the globe.

A PLACE FOR QUESTIONS AND DOUBTS

Teaching extends the discipling ministry to enable the followers of Jesus to mature in their faith and to express their faith commitments in the world. Initially this teaching includes the opportunity to explore and consider the Christian faith among a wide variety of faith options in a pluralistic world. Teachers honor the place of questions and doubts as opportunities to wrestle with the full implications of the gospel or other topic under discussion. Dialogue enables persons to consider loving God with all of one's mind in connection with one's heart, soul, and strength. This fulfills the first of the two great commandments, with the second being fostered in the quality of caring relationships fostered by teachers with students

(Luke 10:27). Knowing that a teacher cares and that expectations are clearly communicated can contribute much to a sense of hope regarding life's journey ahead. Jesus incarnated this hope in his presence with others and his willingness to confront persons with the truth. He did not avoid the costly risks of loving others and being loved in return. The threat of his newly patterned abundant life challenged oppressive structures and forms of relationship. The cross, paradoxically, while signaling the costs and suffering in the crucifix, also in its empty form suggests the victory over death and sin. Teaching in the name of Jesus embraces this paradox and others that life holds in the journey from birth, to death, to life after death. New life intrudes upon that journey in offering glimpses of a hope to be fulfilled in the awaited consummation with a new heaven and earth with Jesus' second coming (Rev 21:1–8).

HOPE EXTENDED

The book of Acts describes the courageous extended teaching ministry of Paul in Ephesus:

> He (Paul) entered the synagogue and for three months spoke out boldly, and argued persuasively about the kingdom of God. When some stubbornly refused to believe and spoke evil of the Way before the congregation, he left them, taking the disciples with him, and argued daily in the lecture hall of Tyrannus. This continued for two years, so that all the residents of Asia, both Jews and Greeks, heard the word of the Lord. (Acts 19:8–10)

Paul persisted in his public teaching in the hall or school of Tyrannus despite the opposition he confronted. This pattern is similar to the teaching of Peter and John in Jerusalem described in Acts 4 and 5. Paul at Ephesus maintained hope with fruitful results. Tyrannus was likely a Greek schoolmaster who allowed Paul use of his setting for teaching. Hope that is extended into the social, communal, and familial dimensions of life becomes prophetic advocacy for those purposes close to the heart of God. Anger is expressed for breaches of the common good of humanity and creation as God intended them to be. Anger is also expressed in the effort to destroy the destroyers of life.[9] Hope is expressed in seeing alternatives to any social order that perpetuates death, terror, fear, greed,

---

9. Gabriel Moran suggests that one of the tasks of religious education is to destroy the destroyers of life. See Moran, *Religious Education Development*, 192.

and acquisition, all at the expense of others. Paul's teaching the word of the Lord at the school of Tyrannus offered an alternative to both Jews and Greeks. Hope extended is often expressed as advocacy. But all advocacies must be tentative to allow for our very real limitations and blindness. I assume that Paul's argumentation at Tyrannus's school for two years included dialogue allowing for the response and questions of his hearers. Humility requires that we recognize our own idolatries and be aware of perspectives other than our cherished own. For teaching, this requires a freedom afforded to others to disagree. A common search for truth holds the possibility of new ventures proposed by both teachers and students.

In the book of Revelation John shares a vision for one venture imagined for all of creation to be renewed and a new humanity realized in the New Jerusalem: "Nothing accursed will be found there any more. But the throne of God and the Lamb will be in it, and his servants will worship him; they will see his face, and his name will be on their foreheads" (Rev 22:3–4). People in the New Jerusalem will worship God and see God face to face with God's name written on their foreheads for all to see. I imagine that the name on foreheads will be that of "Jesus." The bearing of Jesus' name in teaching and learning is fulfilled for all to observe and celebrate.

NEW VENTURES

Teaching is an inherently hopeful ministry. It encourages participants to see, imagine, and dream what God hopes for humanity and all of creation. It offers the possibility of new ventures to those at different points in their life. Participants' experiences and the level of their expertise vary in certain areas of study. The accompanied journey with a teacher over a course of study and reflection holds the promise of new perspectives gained. The promise also includes the opportunity to learn from other participants, if dialogue is practiced and community is nurtured. This ideal is not deterred in maintaining the place for discipline and structure. Both discipline and structure assure boundaries for a journey and avoid fruitless diversion. Here, trust in the experience of the teacher, as an accomplished guide, is a matter for consideration especially in the phase of evaluation. Allowing for evaluation supports the hope that things can be improved or radically changed in the future.

My discussion in this chapter may reflect the hope of a grandfather who longs for a better day for his first grandchild and all grandchildren.

But much more, it represents an abiding assurance of God's active involvement in the human drama from creation to consummation evidenced in the coming and awaited Second Coming of Jesus, God's only begotten Son. This Jesus has begotten through adoption many children and grandchildren of faith of who I am but one. Teachers in their ministry hope that through the time shared with others in learning, lives can be transformed in ways that glorify God and renew the creation. Such transformation is a source of joy that is the topic of our next chapter.

6

Joy and Teaching in the Name of Jesus

A QUESTION THAT CAN be asked of any teaching ministry in any setting or at any level is where is the joy? Joy characterized the teaching ministry of Jesus and can be likewise experienced by his followers. However, how can joy be experienced in the face of suffering, opposition, and contradiction that Christian teachers confront today? The experiences of the earliest followers of Jesus in the book of Acts provide some insights for current-day teaching in his name. Before considering accounts in Acts, a prior question must be asked.

WHAT IS JOY?

Joy is a sense of delight occasioned by God's abiding presence in all of life that leads to awe, reverence, and celebration of life as God's gracious gift. Habakkuk 3:17–19 suggests that joy can transcend the human experiences of success, happiness, or fruitfulness because the source is God:

> Though the fig tree does not blossom, and no fruit is on the vines; though the produce of the olive fails and the fields yield no food; though the flock is cut off from the fold and there is no herd in the stalls, yet I will rejoice in the Lord; I will exult in the God of my salvation. Go, the Lord, is my strength; he makes my feet like the feet of a deer, and makes me tread upon the heights.

C. S. Lewis, in *Surprised By Joy*, distinguishes joy from pleasure and happiness in that joy "is never in our power."[1] Joy is discovered in the ordinary relationships and times of life when a person senses their unity with God that touches the heart, soul, mind, and strength. Joy embraces the gift of God's goodness of shalom with a holistic response of well being

---

1. Lewis, *Surprised By Joy*, 18 and 72. I explore joy related to Christian education in Pazmiño, *Basics of Teaching*, 97–98; and Pazmiño, *God Our Teacher*, 170–71.

and connection at the depths of one's soul. Joy includes the mind with an intellectual embrace of God's care. Joy embraces the heart with an affective resting upon God's sustaining love. Joy invites an intentional/behavioral trust in God's providence and plenitude beyond the circumstances of life. Joy celebrates the wonder of creation and the dignity and worth of persons resting upon God's gracious care.

The Interpreter's Dictionary of the Bible notes: "The experience of joy, as related to praise and thanksgiving in public worship, or to the quiet confidence of the individual in God, or to the proclamation of God's saving power, is one of the characteristic elements in religious faith as described in the Bible."[2] The one difference between Old Testament and New Testament attitudes toward joy is that the New Testament writers go on to the bold statement of joy in suffering as well in salvation. The Old Testament makes clear that a person's cause for rejoicing is in God and not in oneself (Jer 9:23–24). It is in the New Testament that we find the statement of joy in suffering or in weakness seen in terms of a power of God "made perfect in weakness" (Matt 5:12; 2 Cor 12:9)."[3]

The New Testament Dictionary of New Testament Theology notes that joy relates to public occasions of worship and the heart of persons in response to God's help (Ps 13:5). Joy includes an emotion (Ps 16:11); joy in someone or something (2 Sam 1:26; Eccl 11:9); joy in God (Neh 8:10; Ps 33:21); joy in God's word (Jer 15:16; Ps 119:14); joy in keeping the commandments (Ps 119:162); joy in the time of salvation (Isa 35:10). Acts 14:17 speaks of joy in the gifts of nature as being God's gifts in creation. Acts 2:26 and 28, in applying Psalms 16:8–11 to the resurrection, speaks of joy in the presence of God. In Revelation 12:12 and 18:20, joy is eschatological rejoicing and is related to a joyous feast hosted by Jesus. Luke's gospel has joy as one of its basic themes, and the Pauline epistles testify to the paradox that Christian joy is to be found in the midst of sadness, affliction, and care where it gives proof of its power. Therefore the source of this joy is beyond earthly, human joy for it is joy in the Lord as explored in Paul's Letter to the Philippians.[4] These various biblical perspectives provide background to explore the joy in teaching found in the book of Acts.

2. Harvey, "Joy," 1000.

3. Ibid.

4. Beyreuther and Finkenrath, "Joy," 352–61.

Joy and Teaching in the Name of Jesus

BOOK OF ACTS: UNDETERRED JOY IN TEACHING

Acts 5:12–42 records the public teaching outreach of Jesus' apostles following the sobering account of Ananias and Sapphira who sought to deceive the spirit of the Lord (Acts 5:1–11). Great fear seized the whole church in relation to the premature death of this couple that withheld, from God, some of the proceeds of their sale of property. They also sought to deceive others and conceal the truth. In keeping with their reverent fear of God and in response to Jesus' commission (Acts 1:8), the apostles launched a public healing and teaching ministry in Jerusalem. Their public ministry results in their persecution and arrest as ordered by the high priest and their subsequent miraculous release from prison by an angel (Acts 5:19). Upon release, the apostles resume their teaching, telling the people "the whole message about this life" (Acts 5:20) as instructed by the angel of the Lord.

Following their second arrest at the hands of the temple police, the high priest questioned the apostles before the council, saying: "We gave you strict orders not to teach in this name, yet here you have filled Jerusalem with your teaching and you are determined to bring this man's blood on us" (Acts 5:28). Peter and the apostles answered the high priest: "We must obey God rather than any human authority" (Acts 5:29). The council's enraged and murderous response to the apostles was diverted only by the wisdom shared by Gamaliel, a teacher of the law who instructed the apostle Paul. Gamaliel's intervention proposed that the apostles be left alone to discern whether their teaching was of God or of only human origin. The test of time would confirm the divine origin of their teaching. The apostles' release included the council's direct order not to speak or teach in the name of Jesus. As might be expected, the apostles again ignored this order and "every day in the temple and at home they did not cease to teach and proclaim Jesus" (Acts 5:42). This account of the apostles' teaching in the face of strong opposition is a striking example of the joy of teaching in the name of Jesus. It is noted that as the apostles left the council, "they rejoiced that they were considered worthy to suffer dishonor for the sake of the name" (Acts 5:41). The joy of teaching in the name of Jesus and the fruits of persistent faithfulness in this ministry are an encouragement to Christian teachers today.

ACTS 4: THE PRIOR CHALLENGE

The account of Acts 5 is all the more remarkable because it is not the initial encounter of the apostles with direct opposition to their public teaching ministry. Peter and John, recognized as leaders of Jesus' followers, were previously teaching and proclaiming that "in Jesus there is resurrection from the dead" (Acts 4:2). They were arrested and brought before the council in Jerusalem. In this earlier confrontation, Peter and John were ordered "not to speak or teach at all in the name of Jesus" (Acts 4:18). Their recorded response to the council was: "Whether it is right to listen to you rather than to God, you must judge; for we cannot keep from speaking about what we have seen and heard" (Acts 4:19–20). Upon their first release from the council and its threats, Peter and John reported the experience to their friends, including the other apostles. Jesus' followers prayed for boldness in the face of their opposition, and they "were all filled with the Holy Spirit and spoke the word of God with boldness" (Acts 4:31). What can account for the joyful and persistent boldness of Jesus' followers with their teaching in the name of Jesus? What can bring joy to Christian teaching in the face of increased complexity and opposition from a variety of contradictory forces in the wider society and local communities? The accounts of Acts 4 and 5 provide some clues.

In Acts 4, Peter and John were questioned before the assembled council regarding their healing of a crippled beggar (Acts 3:1–10). They were asked: "By what power or by what name did you do this?" (Acts 4:7). Their noteworthy answer was:

> Let it be known to all of you, and all the people of Israel, that this man has been healed by the name of Jesus Christ of Nazareth, whom you crucified, whom God raised from the dead. This Jesus is "the stone that was rejected by you, the builders; it has become the cornerstone." There is salvation in no one else, for there is no other name under heaven by which we must be saved.

The name of Jesus represents the very transformative presence and power of God to bring healing, wholeness, and new life. In Jesus, the fullness of God's revelation and salvation is discovered. That name of Jesus has resounded across the millennia in the teaching and speaking of his followers. God's ultimate plan for creation is disclosed "so that at the name of Jesus every knee should bend, in heaven and on earth and under the earth, and every tongue should confess that Jesus Christ is Lord, to the glory of God the Father" (Phil 2:10–11). The glorious name of Jesus cannot be silenced or squelched, for as Jesus observed in his entry into Jerusalem, even if his disciples were silent, "the stones would shout out" (Luke 19:40).

Public opposition to teaching and speaking in Jesus' name is not unexpected, "for Jews demand signs and Greeks desire wisdom, but we proclaim Christ crucified, a stumbling block to Jews and foolishness to Gentiles, but to those who are called, both Jews and Greeks, Christ the power of God and the wisdom of God" (1 Cor 1:22–24). The opposition confronted by Peter and John, the apostles, and all followers of Jesus throughout the centuries is indicative of what Jesus himself faced in his life, and ultimately culminated in the crucifixion. Paul shares this perspective with the Philippian Christians from his own prison setting in Rome: "I want to know Christ and the power of his resurrection and the sharing of his sufferings by becoming like him in his death, if somehow I may attain the resurrection from the dead" (Phil 3:10–11). Suffering and opposition are not sought out, but faced with the recognition that God's presence and power can sustain Christians. Jesus experienced this same power in his resurrection, and Christians experience it in their diverse trials. In his earthly ministry, Jesus noted the costs of following him when he foretold his death and resurrection: "If any want to become my followers, let them deny themselves and take up their cross daily and follow me" (Luke 9:23).

JOY AMID SUFFERING

Teaching in the name of Jesus is a sobering calling because the example of Jesus poses a challenge for those who shy away from the costs. Nevertheless, the joy of following Jesus transcends the costs of a daily cross and facing the forces of opposition. The writer to the Hebrews encouraged Jesus' followers in the following way:

> Therefore, since we are surrounded by so great a cloud of witnesses, let us also lay aside every weight and sin that clings so closely, and let us run with perseverance the race that is set before us, looking to Jesus the pioneer and perfecter of our faith, who for the sake of the *joy* that was set before him endured the cross, disregarding its shame, and has taken his seat at the right hand of the throne of God. (Heb 12:1–2)

The joy that was set before Jesus was his fulfillment of God's plan for the salvation of humankind and all of creation. Though reluctant to assume the cup of suffering in the cross (Matt 26:39; Mark 14:36; Luke 22:42), Jesus accepted the Father's will over his own. The calling to teach in Jesus' name despite its real costs brings joy in sharing God's wisdom and transformative power with others. Opposition from within oneself in terms of "every weight and sin," as well as opposition from others, cannot squelch the joy in serving the purposes of Christ and God the Father in the world.

THE SPIRIT AS COMPANION

The very spirit of Christ, the Holy Spirit, is the companion of Christian teachers in their ministries. Justo González indicates that "the main character of the book of Acts is the Holy Spirit."[5] The Spirit provides the power, presence, and creative potential to be a source of joy in sharing new and resurrected life with others. This makes all the difference, just as the first followers of Jesus experienced in Jerusalem. They were released from the various prisons and human powers that attempted to forbid their teaching and silence their voices. The Spirit provided a well of joy about which Jesus predicted in his own earthly ministry: "As the scripture has said, 'Out of the believer's heart shall flow rivers of living water.' Now he said this about the Spirit, which believers in him were to receive" (John 7:38–39). The followers of Jesus in Acts 4 and 5 had received the Spirit of whom he spoke at the Pentecost outpouring (Acts 2:1–4). They experienced an additional filling of the Spirit to accomplish their teaching ministries with boldness (Acts 4:31). The Spirit made all the difference in their teaching ministries.

JOY EXTENDED IN CELEBRATION OF FIESTA

Joy extended into the social, communal, and familial dimensions of life becomes festival that in a Latino(a) note is fiesta. The experience of joy is one I have come to celebrate in particular as a member of the Hispanic community. The population increases of the Hispanic community in the United States as documented in the 2000 Census call for a more prominent Hispanic public presence and ministry. Hispanic culture is characterized

---

5. González, *Acts*, 8.

by a predisposition for fiesta, for the public celebration of joy even in the midst of suffering, opposition, and contradiction in life. The suffering of Latinos continues at all levels of public and private life and the passion or *orthopathos*, as named by Samuel Solivan of Hispanic peoples, requires a broader public engagement in teaching and all areas of Christian minis-try.[6] The third millennium provides the occasion to honor the Hispanic heritage among others in the United States. This heritage is one partner in the multicultural celebration of teaching in Jesus' name made possible in the third millennium.[7]

I would maintain that joy is the emotion closest to the heart of God and that our human celebration of joy, in both public worship and festival or fiesta, provides the occasion for our hearts to touch or be in commu-nion with God's heart. Responding to Jesus' call to "follow me" in teach-ing with a sense of adventure and passion increases the joy in following him. Honoring the place of mystery and wonder helps teachers in seeing teaching itself as a sacrament, a form of worship. Teaching in public that fosters a sense of joy can open persons, communities, and societies to new life that God intends for all of creation. Allowing for the play of the Spirit's direction and delight in teaching honors the place of both order and ardor.

A NATION'S JOY

Teachers can open their hearts and lives to become vessels for God's love, laughter, and joy. This openness can surprise and delight others in the process. Fostering humor and hilarity or jubilation in the serendipitous occasions of teaching adds life to the effort. The scriptures describe the potential of communal renewal in the account of Nehemiah 8, where Ezra speaks in the square before the Water Gate and the Levites teach smaller groups of the gathered assembly. Transformation occurs as the people, a nation returning from exile, hear and relate God's word to their corpo-rate and personal lives. Joy infects the whole community and a seven-day fiesta follows as the nation re-appropriates the Festival of the Booths. Ezra pointed out to the people that "the joy of the Lord is your strength"

---

6. Solivan, *Spirit, Pathos and Liberation.*

7. For a discussion of multicultural Christian education see Wilkerson, *Multicultural Religious Education*; James and Lillian Breckenridge, *What Color Is Your God?*; and Conde-Frazier, et al., *Many Colored Kingdom.*

(Neh 8:10). This joy is experienced in the social and communal dimension of life as people celebrate when God restores the nation.

Teaching in the name of Jesus is a joyful challenge for Latinos and all who follow him in their lives and ministries. Mary Elizabeth Molino Moore proposes that as Christians, our calling is to "sacramental teaching—teaching that mediates the Holy, teaching that mediates the grace, power and call of God."[8] This sacramental teaching in the name of Jesus issues in joy for the present and into eternity, recognizing that the chief end of persons is to glorify and enjoy God forever.

As Habakkuk 3:17–19 was noted at the opening of this chapter, I want to return to that passage by sharing a paraphrase I wrote for professional teachers that can also relate to volunteer teachers: "Though the responses are poor and no evidence of learning is apparent, though the lesson plans fail and the curriculum needs extensive revision, though the students are absent, yet I will rejoice in the Lord, I will be joyful in God my Savior."[9] Alan M. McPherson, a pastor, suggests that "the defining characteristic of the life of faith is joy." Even in times of loss and suffering as Habakkuk suggested, "our hearts can rejoice in the love, peace, and faithful promises of the Lord."[10] These hold true for the ministry of teaching and are a source of joy unceasing and full of glory.

CONCLUSION

Teaching in the name of Jesus is a high calling. Despite the current devaluing of teaching in society, it holds the promise of transforming persons, families, communities, and the wider society. Neglect of its potential has led to the demise of persons and communities for whom Jesus himself died. Communities that have failed to invest adequately in its teaching ministries with time, dedication, and resources have suffered decline over time. Jesus' exemplary model incarnated the five virtues of truth, love, faith, hope, and joy that can sustain teaching over the centuries with vision and vitality. He incarnated these virtues in his life with humility that called for his crucifixion and resurrection.

Teaching in Jesus' names calls for the wholehearted response of Christians gifted and called to teach. Bearing the name of Jesus in the

8. Moore, "Sacramental Teaching," 41.

9. Pazmiño, Basics of Teaching, 98.

10. McPherson, "Sheer Joy."

third millennium places Christian teachers in a long tradition of persons who have shared their lives along with their teachings in the life of the church. The tradition is living and transformative because of the partnership with the Holy Spirit and other pilgrims who follow in the steps of the Master Teacher. Here is the source of joy to sustain each and every Christian teacher in her or his current and future ministries.

A source of joy for my wife and I is spending time with Oliver, our grandson, to whom this book is dedicated. Oliver bears our family name of Pazmiño, but he also bears some resemblance to me as we compare family photos from when I was his age. The invitation to teach in the name of Jesus calls for resembling Jesus in the virtues he exemplified of truth, love, faith, hope, and joy all held with humility in serving our Lord. We also resemble Jesus by teaching in his spirit that is the focus of part two.

PART TWO

Teaching in the Spirit of Jesus

A GREAT INTEREST IN spirituality in relation to life and teaching persists in current discussions. In 1983, the seminal work of Parker Palmer, *To Know As We Are Known: A Spirituality of Education*, extended the persistent Christian concern for spiritual matters into the public realm of educational discourse.[1] A theme issue of the journal *Educational Leadership* in December 1998 addressed the topic, "The Spirit of Education," and Palmer wrote its initial feature article, "Evoking the Spirit in Public Education."[2] While celebrating the universal educational interest in spiritual and religious matters, questions of particularity may loom for Christian educators. Just what spirit do we hope to invoke and how do we discern the spirits in teaching and learning in this age of religious plurality? More specifically: What, if anything, is distinct about the spirit of Jesus or the Holy Spirit in teaching? Christians can affirm the presence of God's Spirit in all of creation and diverse religious traditions, yet also wonder about the particularities of following Jesus in teaching today.

Christian educators have contributed to the task of discerning spiritual dynamics in the tradition of Jesus. In 1972 Roy Zuck wrote *Spiritual Power in Your Teaching* to explore the role of the Holy Spirit in teaching.[3] Iris Cully explored the cultivation of spiritual life through the processes on nurture and education in *Education for Spiritual Growth*.[4] Perry Downs, in *Teaching for Spiritual Growth*, explores two questions: What does it mean to be spiritually mature? What can the church do to help people

1. Palmer, *Know As We Are Known*.
2. Palmer, "Evoking the Spirit," 6–11.
3. Zuck, *Spiritual Power in Your Teaching*.
4. Cully, *Education for Spiritual Growth*.

grow spiritually?[5] Each author affirms the crucial role of the Holy Spirit in teaching. Christian educators, in turn, are called to be responsive to the teaching of the Spirit and to recognize that the Spirit guides persons "into all truth" (John 16:13). If teaching is seen as one essential expression of "speaking the truth in love" (Eph 4:15), then the Spirit's guidance is indispensable for the teaching task and for any learning that is hoped for as a fruit of that teaching. The discovery of truth is not limited to the ministry of teaching because persons learn outside of their direct relationship with teachers in a wide variety of ways. But if Christian teaching has the intent of fostering the transformation of persons through their learning, the Spirit's presence and ministry is crucial.

The implicit challenge for the Christian teacher is how to set the metaphorical table for the Holy Spirit in one's teaching. If the Spirit is like the wind, how can the Spirit be directed and channeled in faithful ways? One response is to recognize the mystery of the Spirit's work and to allow room or space for that covert ministry in each phase of teaching. In my work *Basics of Teaching for Christians*, I considered the Spirit's ministry in the preparation, instruction, and evaluation phases of teaching.[6] This requires the conscious dependence upon prayer in each teaching phase and willingness, along with careful planning, to allow for flexibility. The Spirit, as well as the wind, brings surprises that call for a response of wonder and awe in the ordinary and special events of our lives. A careful assessment of Jesus' first miracle at Cana, recorded in chapter 2 of the gospel of John, provides insights for understanding the person and work of the Spirit in ministry and teaching. Jesus' spirit was present in his person at the special event of a wedding. Second Corinthians 3:17 teaches us: "Now the Lord is the Spirit, and where the Spirit of the Lord is, there is freedom." This freedom to respond to human need as exemplified by Jesus and summoned by Mary is the focus of chapter seven. In chapter eight the Spirit's presence in contemporary teaching is explored. The gospel of John describes one of Jesus' post-resurrection appearances where he shares with his disciples these words: "Jesus said to them again, 'Peace be with you. As the Father has sent me, so I send you.' When he said this, he breathed on them and said to them, 'Receive the Holy Spirit' " (John 20:21–22). Christian

5. Downs, *Teaching for Spiritual Growth*.
6. Pazmiño, *Basics of Teaching*.

teachers today have received the spirit of Jesus, and with this gift, comes the freedom to minister with persons across the life span.

7

The Spirit Present at Cana

T HE GOSPEL OF JOHN begins the account of Jesus' public teaching ministry with his presence at the wedding feast in Cana:

> On the third day there was a wedding in Cana of Galilee, and the
> mother of Jesus was there. Jesus and his disciples had also been
> invited to the wedding. When the wine gave out, the mother of
> Jesus said to him, "They have no wine." And Jesus said to her,
> "Woman, what concern is that to you and me? My hour has not
> yet come." His mother said to the servants, "Do whatever he tells
> you." Now standing there were six stone water jars for the Jewish
> rites of purification, each holding twenty or thirty gallons. Jesus
> said to them, "Fill the jars with water." And they filled them up
> to the brim. He said to them, "Now draw some out, and take it to
> the chief steward." So they took it. When the steward tasted the
> water that had become wine, and did not know where it came from
> (though the servants who had drawn the water knew), the steward
> called the bridegroom and said to him, "Everyone serves the good
> wine first, and then the inferior wine after the guests have become
> drunk. But you have kept the good wine until now." Jesus did this,
> the first of his signs, in Cana of Galilee, and revealed his glory; and
> his disciples believed in him. (John 2:1–11)

This account provides insights into the very person of Jesus and his response to persons in his earthly journey. The spirit of Jesus' ministry is captured in both his actions and those with whom he interacts on this joyous occasion of a marriage feast. Jesus taught through his presence and interactions at this event. A number of theological themes emerge from the account and these provide insights for the ministry of teaching. Jesus, in his own person as the incarnated Son of God, provides normative categories with which to assess Christian education. I propose that Jesus' first miracle is a model for his care of persons in life and its transitions.

The presence of the imaginative and creative spirit of Christ in the caring for persons across the life span has implications for teaching that will be explored further in chapter eight.

How can teachers today be like Jesus in their teaching? How are they different from the example of Jesus' teaching ministry in the first century? In focusing upon persons with the spirit of Jesus identified as the Holy Spirit, a response to these questions of comparison can hinge a great deal upon how persons may or may not have changed between the first- and twenty-first centuries. The additional factor relates to the particular person of Jesus and how he is similar and/or different from teachers today.

THE GLORY OF JESUS

The major theological theme of this Johannine passage is the glory of Jesus and his person (v. 11), as the New Testament scholar Raymond E. Brown suggests in his commentary of this gospel. Jesus is the Son of God sent to bring salvation to the world in its great need. The response of his disciples is to believe in him (v. 11). What shines through this Johannine account is Jesus' glory, and his disciples' reaction of belief in this striking revelation.[1] The glory of Jesus' person reflects upon the person and worth of all those identified in this account and all of humanity. At this joyful occasion of marriage, Jesus' mother, Mary, identifies a need: "They have no wine" (v. 3). The lack of wine noticed by Mary may have been occasioned by the arrival of Jesus and his disciples. They added to the gathering and, in part, created a desperate problem for those hosting the wedding. The lack of wine would have been an embarrassment to all participants and squelched the joy of the event. The failure to have sufficient wine would have caused acute shame for the family, particularly at a marriage supper. Mary confronted Jesus with the need for wine, but Jesus sets the boundary of both his person and his response. Each person, beginning with Jesus in this account, needs to respect their own person and God's particular calling in their lives. Others may propose a number of alternatives and many good things to do at their timing, but a sense of integrity for each person involves the setting of boundaries and choices referenced to one's particular calling, as Jesus modeled at Cana.

The account of a wedding itself discloses the interaction of persons and, in particular, families, as weddings involve the commitment and union

1. Brown, *Gospel According to John*, 103–4.

of two families. Having officiated and hosted at my son's wedding in 2001 and officiated at my sister's wedding in November of 2006, I have a sense of these real-life dynamics. The interaction of Jesus and his mother does not suggest any hint of disrespect on Jesus' part in relation to his mother's request to respond to the immediate crisis of no wine. Jesus respected the person of his mother. Brown points out that Jesus' form of addressing his mother as "woman," in the text, "is not a rebuke, nor an impolite term, nor an indication of a lack of affection (in 19:26 the dying Jesus uses it for Mary again). It was Jesus' normal, polite way of addressing women (Matt 15:28; Luke 13:12; John 4:21, 8:10, 20:13)."[2] But Brown points up that Mary does seem to expect some answer or action on Jesus' part to the human dilemma of no wine on this special occasion. Jesus, in response to Mary's expectation, "always insists that human kinship, whether it be Mary's or that of his disbelieving relatives (John 7:1–10), cannot affect the pattern of his ministry, for he has his father's work to do."[3] Adoption into God's family is to have a higher priority over family ties. Jesus' response suggests a clear demarcation of independence in relation to his mother's, and more broadly, family's, expectations. Yet it also indicates his relationship of interdependence with the gathered group in supplying an abundance of good or choice wine for the joyful wedding event. Interdependence is also suggested in relation to Jesus' reliance upon God his Father in that his hour had not yet come. The "hour" is the "technical Johannine term referring to the period of the passion, death, resurrection, and ascension" of Jesus and it is reiterated in John 7:6, 8, 30, and 8:20.[4] Further references to the "hour" in John 12:23, 24; 13:1; 17:1 and 2 clarify the significance for Jesus' earthly ministry as appointed by his Father.

THE SPIRIT?

Without any explicit mention of the spirit of Jesus or the Holy Spirit, the reader can justifiably question the title of this chapter. Later in John's gospel, Jesus explicitly promises the coming of the Spirit to guide his followers into all truth (John 14:15–31; 15:26–27; 16:4–15).[5] For the author

2. Ibid., 99.

3. Ibid., 102.

4. Ibid., 99–100.

5. Ibid., see Brown's discussion of the Holy Spirit in John's gospel as "Paraclete" in 2:1135–44.

the spirit of adoption into God's family is implied in how Jesus responds to human need and how he defines his relationships with other persons. Clearly in relationship with his mother, he noted a higher calling to the agenda set for him by his Father, including his decisions and actions. The appointed hour of his revelation was not determined by his mother Mary's expectations and request. Jesus' response to the obvious need for wine is set on his terms and the gracious obedience of the servants present at the wedding feast. It is noteworthy that the servants are knowledgeable about the source of the good or choice wine served near the end of the feast when its quality might remain unnoticed. The chief steward and bridegroom do not know from the account recorded in John's gospel. The other participants who gained knowledge of the true source of good wine in abundance are Jesus' disciples. As a result of their witnessing the miracle of water changed into wine that revealed Jesus' glory, they believe in him. Belief as a gift of God's Spirit is the hoped-for response to the glorious revelation of Jesus. This stands in stark contrast with the waters of purification, even when filled to the jars' brims, that cannot address the need for wine to celebrate the formation of a new family. Jesus' presence allows for the transformation of the water into wine. The wine in abundance suggests the new covenant Jesus offers in his blood once the hour (referring to his death) is fulfilled in his mission occasioned by his passion, death, and resurrection later recorded in John's gospel. Jesus' person and spirit transform the ordinary water for cleansing into the wine of celebration. At the close of Luke's gospel, the foretaste of Jesus' spirit enjoyed here at Cana is promised to his followers at Pentecost: "And see, I am sending upon you what the father promised: so stay here in the city until you have been clothed with power from on high" (Luke 24:49).

FOUR THEOLOGICAL THEMES

Brown identifies four theological themes from the Cana passage that are insightful for teaching in the spirit of Jesus. The four themes are the glory of Jesus revealed; the call of disciples completed; the symbolism of Mary as the mother of Jesus; and the choice wine representing the Eucharist or Lord's Supper. The first of these four themes is the most prominent and deserves the most attention as affirmed in the passage itself.[6] My

6. Brown, *Gospel According to John*, 103–10.

discussion explores each of these themes from the perspective of Christian education.

The Glory of Jesus

The glory of Jesus revealed affirms the person of Jesus himself fulfilling the call of God and the timing of God for his earthly ministry. In the Old Testament the Holy Spirit is associated with the Shekinah Glory of God's dwelling with God's people now present in Jesus himself. As Christian teachers we can ask ourselves: How does ordinary teaching take on a new dimension in the presence of Jesus? How is Jesus' glory evident in our teaching? The person of Jesus reveals the fullness of God incarnate. Jesus' presence at the wedding feast and his response to the need for wine suggests "messianic replacement and abundance"[7] satisfying human needs. Brown explains from the perspective of a host of signs regarding Jesus' uniqueness in John's gospel:

> Jesus is the real Temple; the Spirit he gives will replace the necessity of worshipping at Jerusalem; his doctrine and flesh and blood give life in a way that the manna associated with the exodus from Egypt did not; at Tabernacles, not the rain-making ceremony but Jesus himself supplies the living water; not the illumination in the temple court but Jesus himself is the real light; on the feast of dedication; not the temple altar but Jesus himself is consecrated by God. In view of this consistent theme of replacement, it seems obvious that, in introducing Cana as the first in a series of signs to follow, the evangelist intends to call attention to the replacement of the water prescribed for Jewish purification by the choicest of wines. This replacement is a sign of who Jesus is, namely the one sent by the Father who is now the only way to the Father. All previous religious institutions, customs and feasts lose meaning in his presence.[8]

In light of the disclosure of Jesus' person and his gracious offer to humankind, the ordinary and popular occasion of a wedding takes on extraordinary character. Persons are surprised by joy with the abundance of choice wine at a time when it is not expected in the normal progression of such a wedding event. God's grace extends far beyond what persons expect in life. Nevertheless, this miraculous disclosure can assist persons

7. Ibid., 104.
8. Ibid.

73

to see God's presence in the ordinary and everyday affairs of life when water is transformed into wine as the gift of creation. C. S. Lewis, the most influential lay theologian of the twentieth century, makes this connection in his commentary on miracles:

> This miracle proclaims that the God of all wine is present. The vine is one of the blessings sent by Yahweh: He is the reality behind the false god Bacchus. Every year, as part of the Natural order, God makes wine. He does so by creating a vegetable organism that can turn water, soil, and sunlight into a juice, which will, under proper conditions, become wine. Thus, in a certain sense, He constantly turns water into wine, for wine, like all drinks, is but water modified. Once, and in one year only, God, now incarnate, short-circuits the process: makes wine in a moment: uses earthenware jars instead of vegetable fibres to hold the water. But uses them to do what He is always doing. The Miracle consists in the short cut; but the event to which it leads is the usual one. If the thing happened, then we know that what has come into Nature is no anti-Natural spirit, no God who loves tragedy and tears and fasting *for their own sake* (however He may permit or demand them for special purposes) but the God of Israel has through all these centuries given us wine to gladden the hearts of man.[9]

Lewis, as a theologian, captures the wonder and glory of God's grace in our ordinary life that Jesus' miracle makes possible. This wonder extends to the wonder of each person and the wonder of human life and love that finds one expression in the wedding of two persons.

The joy of Jesus' coming and the salvation he offers extends into all of life, making it qualitatively different. God takes on human flesh and provides a fulfillment for persons prefigured in the creation, made complete in the new creation. This is a source of great joy reflected in the occasion of a wedding. Personally I had some sense of this joy when officiating at the wedding ceremony of my son, and participating with the children while they danced at the wedding reception. I have had the privilege of officiating at other wedding services for extended family and friends, but halfway through my son and daughter-in-law's ceremony I sensed a difference. The family and guests assembled noticed the difference in my voice when I realized that this was my very son who was committed to establish a new family with my new daughter. Recounting the event

---

9. Lewis, *Five Best Books*, 333–34.

brings a sense of joy as when I view the gift of their wedding album, and as I thank God for the memories and shared life that now includes the gift of a grandchild (Ps 128:6). God's glory is revealed in Jesus, and his person, and his presence in all the dimensions of life. Teaching can foster a sense of this glory for all to enjoy even in the ordinary and in daily routines. Fostering a sense of wonder is a potential for transformative teaching as persons in the first- and twenty-first centuries attend to God's grace in their lives.

Think for Ourselves at Wisdom's Table

Brown's second theological theme, the call of the disciples completed, in the Cana account indicates that Jesus encouraged his followers or students to think for themselves. While issuing a clear call for persons to follow him, Jesus respected the persons of followers in relation to their commitments. This suggests the need for teachers to present options and expect choices to be made by those participating. Doing so respects the freedom of thought, affection, and will gifted to humanity by God but impacted by the realities of sin and its consequences.[10] The disclosure of wisdom in the person and teaching of Jesus demands a response. Brown relates the offering of wisdom to key Old Testament passages that have richly informed my reflections on Christian education.[11] Proverbs 9:1–6 describes wisdom's feast now found complete in Jesus "in whom are hidden all the treasures of wisdom and knowledge" (Col 2:3). Isaiah 55:1–3 extends an invitation to dine that offers wine, milk, and bread that ultimately fulfill human hungers and deepest needs. Brown points up:

> The act of dining at Wisdom's table and drinking her wine is a symbol for accepting her message. The Wisdom motif will be clear in ch. vi where Jesus is the bread of life who feeds men with doctrine—a scene set in Galilee just before Passover (vi 4). Here, at Cana in Galilee just before Passover (ii 13), we have Jesus giving men wine in abundance to drink, and this leads his disciples to

10. For a discussion of sin and salvation related to teaching see Pazmiño, *God Our Teacher*, 37–57.

11. See Pazmiño, *God Our Teacher*, 26; and Pazmiño, *Basics of Teaching*, 11–12, where I define teaching as "artfully setting an inviting table that welcomes all to participate and results in joyful celebration."

believe in him ... It is not the bread and wine of the Law that feeds
men, but Jesus himself, the incarnation of divine Wisdom.[12]

Being at the table is one response, but the choice to partake suggests receptivity with the ingestion and digestion of what is offered. This
denotes completion of the call to discipleship. For teaching this implies
the need to foster the whole life response and commitment to that which
is taught, engaging the head, heart, and hands.

Mary as an Example

Brown's third theme, Mary as the mother of Jesus, poses a particular challenge for Protestants like the author, but less so for Orthodox and Catholic
Christians. Catholic Christians affirm the crucial role of Mary as one who
bore God's new life. I think in their veneration of her ministry, some
Catholics overstate her efficacy. Nevertheless, Protestants in the twenty-
first century can appreciate that she models a level of commitment and
discipleship former generations have ignored. Brown points up that "from
the earliest days of Christianity Mary was seen as both a symbol of the
Church and the New Eve."[13]

As a symbol of the Church, Mary's request for help with the wine
leads to Jesus' response in performing the miracle of transforming water
into wine. But Brown notes that "before he does perform this sign, Jesus
must make clear his refusal of Mary's intervention; she cannot have any
role in his ministry; his signs must reflect his father's sovereignty, and
not any human, or family agency."[14] The limits to Mary's, and by implication the Church's, role in God's plans and mission require clarification.
Compliance and obedience to God's will are priorities in Christian mission, including the mission of teaching. With this clarification, Mary still
serves as an example of Christian discipleship and commitment from the
beginning of Jesus' life in her womb (John 1:14; Luke 1:38), to the first
public disclosure of his ministry (John 2:1–11), and to his death upon the
cross (John 19:25–27). Even in the Cana account Mary is encouraging
others, the servants in this case, to do whatever Jesus tells them (John
2:5). Ironically, Jesus did make the absence of wine a concern diserving
his response as Mary had suggested. Here is a criterion for Christian

12. Brown, *Gospel According to John*, 106–7.
13. Ibid., 108.
14. Ibid., 109.

discipleship and teaching as suggested in Matthew 28:16–20 that is the great educational commission for the Church, namely obeying all that Jesus teaches and requests in our lives.

The Choice Wine of the Lord's Provision

Brown's fourth theological theme highlights the choice wine of Cana as representing the Eucharist or Lord's Supper. He points out the subtle sacramentality: "Though the water for Jewish purifications is replaced, it is not replaced by the waters of Christian Baptism but by wine." Whereas the hour at Cana had not come, in John 13:1 the appointed hour of Jesus' suffering, death, and resurrection had come, making the Eucharistic connection with Cana.[15] Teaching provides the occasion to incarnate Christian virtues as explored in part one, and it can represent a sacrament offered to God in Christ for the repair and advance of the world. A sacrament is a vehicle of God's grace. Teaching can be an expression of thanksgiving or Eucharist that flows from a life of loving service as exemplified by Jesus. Teaching also holds the potential of bringing new life and joy, as it becomes a vehicle in the hands of the spirit of Jesus. The Spirit is alive and well in the lives of all those who follow after Jesus in their teaching today. James Michael Lee elaborates upon the sacramental dimensions of teaching. He defines a sacrament as:

> [A] ritual that enacts, focuses, and concentrates the distinctive beliefs, affects, and lifestyle of a particular religious tradition. A sacrament constitutes the surpassing exemplar and overarching paradigm for all other holy acts that take place in that religion. A sacrament bears a privileged relationship both to that religious tradition as a whole and to the specific activities that occur within that tradition.[16]

Lee proposes that teaching itself be viewed as a sacrament in the light of the great educational commission of Matthew 28:18–20 that affirms teaching as "a surpassing exemplar and overarching paradigm within which all other activities within Christianity take place."[17] Jesus teaching is exemplary and provides the norm by which the followers of

---

15. Ibid., 110.

16. Lee, *Sacrament of Teaching*, 21. For a recent work that explores the theological roots of Lee's approach, see Newell, *"Education Has Nothing to Do with Theology."*

17. Ibid.

Jesus evaluate their teaching.[18] Jesus incarnates the best of what teaching should be. Mary Magdalene recognized this reality in John 20:16, where at the resurrection she refers to Jesus as *Rabbouni* (Teacher).

To return to the question posed at the beginning of this chapter comparing persons in the first- and twenty-first centuries, one answer can affirm the commonalties and continuities. Persons need to be affirmed in their own identities that from a faith perspective recognizes their particular callings. Jesus' response to his mother asserted his personhood. At the same time, persons are members of the human community that calls for recognition of interdependence. Individuality cannot descend into a destructive individualism devoid from the community; that represents one danger. A second danger exists with the loss of individuality in a destructive communalism. The first danger is one most applicable to cultures of the north and west globally, and the second to cultures of the south and east. Teaching seeks to balance the recognition of individual persons with their relationships in the wider communities of human interaction. Jesus responded on his terms in accord with his appointed hour to the need for wine. He was not subject to his mother's timing. Nevertheless, Jesus relied upon the actions of the servants to make available to all at the wedding feast the water transformed into wine. The servants filled the jars to the brim with water, drew it out, and took it to the chief steward. Balancing particularity with universality and individuality with community is a challenge in the encounters of everyday life. Jesus at Cana modeled for teachers today the interaction with others that maintains one's personal integrity. Jesus, initially a guest at the wedding, in response to a real need becomes the host in providing wine.[19] The spirit present at Cana honors this dynamic of abundant life and gladness with which Jesus came to bless humanity represented in the wine gifted to all the wedding party and guests.

CONCLUSION

In conclusion, it is helpful to return to the four theological themes identified by Brown. First, teaching can reveal the glory of God amid the ordinary and extraordinary routines of encouraging the learning of others.

18. See my discussion of Jesus' exemplary teaching role in Pazmiño, *God Our Teacher*, 59–86.

19. Pineda, "Hospitality," 34.

Second, teaching can be a vehicle through which God calls disciples and helps them discern the fullness of their discipleship. Third, teaching can foster the independence of persons and their interdependence within the entire human community. Fourth, teaching can be a sacramental vehicle for fostering the joyful care of persons as an expression of God's grace in the world today. Teaching can be a vehicle for the ministry of the Spirit as it was at Cana. Christian teachers are called to recognize their humble and utter dependence upon God. In responding to a public presentation of this work my good colleague Kevin Lawson insightfully observed the following: "All I have is water when I come to teach. Jesus must transform it into wine." Chapter eight explores this potential in our contemporary setting.

8

The Spirit Present in Contemporary Teaching

WHAT OF THE SPIRIT of Jesus captured in the description of his first miracle at Cana can possibly apply to contemporary teaching? Chapter seven made a number of suggestions in response to such a question by building upon four theological themes, including Jesus' glory, the call of discipleship, human and divine relationships, and the sacrament of teaching itself. The task of this eighth chapter is broader in scope. Specifically how can teachers today discern the person and work of Jesus' spirit, the Holy Spirit, in fulfilling their calling in the third millennium as compared with Jesus' first millennium ministry?

RESPONSIVENESS TO PERSONS

One enduring quality of Jesus' spirit that is applicable for teaching today is his responsiveness to persons with their genuine needs. The mention of *genuine* or *real* needs as compared with *felt* needs is crucial. The Jewish educator Abraham Heschel made this explicit in his warning about the "tyranny of needs" that can plague contemporary perceptions.[1] By this term, Heschel referred to the cultural development whereby felt needs become holy to the relative exclusion of God's demands and human responsibilities. Wants fueled by the idolatries and excesses of consumerism become equated with needs to the peril of creation and its care. Needs identified in typical educational planning require spiritual discernment to maintain faithfulness to Jesus' legacy and spirit. A German pastor and theological educator shared an example of this challenge in describing the request for funds for a youth event in his ministry. To attract youth, the request came for funds to travel to Norway. In the past, youth events held in special and spacious locations in the former East Germany were more

1. Heschel, *Between God and Man*, 129–51; see also Gross, *Educating to Reverence*.

than sufficient in building a sense of community and spiritual growth among youth. Norway is an attractive setting for a visit, but the notion was shared that the youth needed an extravagant and costly trip to justify their participation and Christian formation. A costly tourism is not the domain of only youth, but can apply to adults as well in educational planning. Clarity with regard to the spiritual purposes and costs of programs in relation to education, formation, transformation, and mission is essential.

SPIRITUAL MATTERS

Raising the matter of spiritual purposes and discernment in Christian teaching requires direct consideration of the person and work of the Holy Spirit. In my work *God Our Teacher*, I devote one chapter to discuss God in us in terms of the Spirit's presence and guidance in teaching.[2] Beyond that discussion, it is crucial for teachers to identify the genuine or real needs that affect persons. The Holy Spirit works in partnership with the spirits of teachers to identify and address those needs. The Spirit works in and through the lives and teaching of Christian educators to inform, form, and transform persons. In 1 Thessalonians 2:8 the apostle Paul suggests such in his words describing his first-century teaching ministry: "So deeply do we care for you that we are determined to share with you not only the gospel of God but also our own selves because you have become very dear to us." In commenting on 1 Thessalonains 2:1–12, the New Testament scholar Abraham Smith indicates that the teacher/student relationship deserves special attention. Teachers are to exemplify "a passionate commitment to teaching the truth," as explored in chapter two of this work, and careful attention to "the differing needs of each student," as explored in chapter three.[3] In Paul's words recorded to his disciple Timothy this is reiterated in 1 Timothy 4:16: "Pay close attention to yourself and to your teaching; continue in these things, for in doing this you will save both yourself and your hearers." Attention to the teaching and one's life is crucial to Timothy's ministry and to the ministry of Christian teachers today. Faithfulness to the teaching is linked with salvation and as James Dunn comments: "The strength is that the teaching does encapsulate what Christians have found

---

2. Pazmiño, *God Our Teacher*, 87–112.
3. Smith, "First Letter to the Thessalonians," 701.

from the start to contain the words of life."[4] The example of one's life as a teacher needs to support the content of one's teaching. James 3:1 issues a warning in relation to that connection: "Not many of you should become teachers, my brothers and sisters, for you know that we who teach will be judged with greater strictness." Therefore spiritual discernment is personally required of the teacher before discerning the needs of the participants in any teaching ministry.

Teachers are also called to exercise spiritual discernment in each of the three phases of teaching that I identify as preparation, instruction, and evaluation.[5] A teacher's prayer life and attentive listening to all participants foster spiritual discernment. In addition, a teacher must exercise sensitivity to a variety of contextual factors. James 1:5 provides a practical suggestion to guide the teacher's prayer life: "If any of you is lacking in wisdom, ask God, who gives generously and ungrudgingly, and it will be given you." This suggestion holds the gracious promise of God's wisdom to guide the teaching in following the spirit of Jesus.

JESUS OUR EXEMPLAR?

In suggesting the following of Jesus' spirit a question emerges: How is this the case if Jesus was divine and distinct from human teachers today? Klaus Issler addresses this question as he responds to another question in proposing Jesus as a model today: How human was or is Jesus? He suggests that "Jesus walked and talked using *solely* his own human powers, without any recourse to his own divine powers, but relying on the divine power of the Holy Spirit."[6] If Jesus serves as an exemplar for Christian teachers as I suggest, then Christian teachers need to rely upon the Spirit's wisdom, anointing, working, and power to be effective today. This spirit of adoption (Rom 8:15–17) enables teachers to appropriate God's resources for the tasks and activities of teaching. Being adopted into God's triune family affords Christian teachers the rights and privileges along with the obligations of this relationship and lifelong connection. The conscious practice of this connection with God in Christ through the Spirit calls

4. Dunn, "First and Second Letters," 815.

5. Pazmiño, *Basics of Teaching*.

6. Issler, "Spiritual Formation of Jesus," 13–14. This is clear in Jesus' first public teaching where in the synagogue at Nazareth he notes his reliance upon the Spirit's anointing for his ministry (Luke 4:14–21).

for discipline and a willingness to devote time for such a relationship. In a time of "quick fixes" and shallow answers to long-term matters, an alternative is demanded for Christian discipleship. The nurture and formation of faithful teaching service requires attention to one's teaching and life as noted in both Paul's example among the Thessalonians and his admonition to Timothy.

THE SPIRIT TODAY

In exploring the Spirit present in contemporary teaching the best option is to consider the persons with whom one is teaching. Teaching intends to foster the learning of other persons, so careful consideration of those persons is crucial for effectiveness in teaching itself. It can be further suggested that teachers themselves need to model the joy for learning in their practice and life. Jesus modeled for teachers today his deep and intimate care for persons. Persons were respected for themselves and valued as having an intrinsic worth and dignity. Jesus also expected persons to become and be all that God intended. This implied the liberation of persons from all that limited their experience of the abundant life God intends for humanity and all of creation. Such liberation includes personal, communal, and societal dimensions that give expression to the new spiritual life Jesus offers through his own life, death, and resurrection. In exploring the spirit of Jesus manifested through the variety of teaching ministries today, it helps to focus on the particular needs of children, youth, and adults, along with their common life shared in families and communities. Educational planning requires the consideration of how and when persons are both huddled together with a particular age group and mixed across age groups to support their learning. The informal learning that makes up everyday life always complements any formal and nonformal learning. In an age-segregated society the mixing of age groups needs to be intentional considering the fragmented nature of both modern and postmodern life. Local church and family experiences may be the remaining vestiges of intergenerational learning opportunities for many children and youth. These opportunities are suggestive for intentional planning in faith formation for the rising generations. What can be suggested for children, youth, adults, families, and church communities that capture the teaching spirit of Jesus today?

CHILDREN

Jesus modeled the inclusion of children in faith formation and the honoring of their ministries as the oft quoted words from Luke 18:16–17 indicate: "Let the little children come to me, and do not stop them; for it is to such as these that the kingdom of God belongs. Truly I tell you, whoever does not receive the kingdom of God as a little child will never enter it."[7] Children are clearly valued as active members of faith communities and are to be protected as suggested by Jesus' recorded words of sober warning regarding them:

> Whoever becomes humble like this child is the greatest in the kingdom of heaven. Whoever welcomes one such child in my name welcomes me. If any of you put a stumbling block before one of these little ones who believe in me, it would be better for you if a great millstone were fastened around your neck and you were drowned in the depth of the sea. Woe to the world because of stumbling blocks! Occasions for stumbling are bound to come, but woe to the one by whom the stumbling block comes! (Matt 18:4–7)

The responsibility in caring for children is one that relates to the entire community with special obligations for parents and/or the primary caregivers. Children represent the present and ongoing legacy of a faith community and the allocation of resources should honor their importance and their ministries. When much distracts from societal, communal, and familial priorities, the basic needs of children are a matter for constant advocacy for all believers.

In the United States, a great debt is owed to the efforts of the Children's Defense Fund in raising awareness of the gaps in the care for children, and globally to the work of UNICEF. Beyond these public efforts, local churches and voluntary associations have crucial ministries to sustain a full and secure life for all children. The teaching of faith with children requires the honoring of their particular gifts offered to the entire community. I have had the privilege of professionally working with emotionally disturbed children and recently of grandparenting my first grandchild. These experiences, full of wonder and challenge, invite a renewed sense of public accountability for all children's needs globally. Lesser

---

7. For one key work on the inclusion of children, see Mercer, *Welcoming Children*.

commitments daily continue to ravage the lives of younger persons created in the image of God and worthy of care and respect.

The investment in the Christian education of children holds a promise: "Train children in the right way, and when old, they will not stray" (Prov 22:6). The challenge implied in this text is for teachers to discern the right way applicable to individual children with a wide diversity of learning styles, "multiple intelligences," gifts, abilities, interests, and dispositions. Prayer is crucial, along with the counsel and support of others, to teach children in the ways of God applicable to their particular world with the stumbling blocks Jesus noted. A challenge in working with children is how to balance form and freedom in the teaching setting. Structure, activity, and discipline provide form. Care, patience, and advocacy provide freedom. Both form and freedom are needed to support the growth and development of children.

YOUTH

Youth, like children, are to be valued as present participants in the life of the faith community, and less as only potential future contributors and leaders. Youth can effectively serve as leaders and prophets in the life of church because they embrace cultural shifts and are very adept at citing the gaps between our stated intentions and actual practices in faith communities. The example of the youthful Jesus himself, in Luke 2:41–52, is noteworthy as he interacted with the teachers in the temple. The teaching pattern of asking questions, listening, and sharing insights at the temple is one that is remarkably repeated at the close of Jesus' ministry on the road to Emmaus (Luke 24:13–35).[8]

Youth in postmodern times confront a vast array of choices that complicates the exploration of their identity. Strong mentoring relationships can support the journey into young adulthood with the increased fragmentation of extended families and local communities. The rise of peer and gang associations too often can fill the gap in dysfunctional ways. The investment in youth ministry at the parachurch or church level is worth the best efforts of all Christians who have a stake in the perpetuation of the faith across generations. This passing on of the faith is required from biblical sources like Deuteronomy 6 and Psalm 78 that call for the integration of faith and life. Youth not only pose a challenge for churches

8. See Pazmiño, *Latin American Journey*, xi–xii.

that resist change, but also need to be challenged themselves to fulfill God's calling for their lives as a part of a living faith tradition. From my six-year ministry with youth in East Harlem, New York, I was awed by the difference active youth made in the process of renewing congregational life and communal outreach efforts that were sustained over time. The energy and vision of youth provide a potential for discerning how the faith addresses new cultural and societal shifts that have informed their perspectives. The partnership of youth with other age groups can become vehicles for the spirit of Jesus to incarnate new ministry possibilities. Such new efforts cannot ignore the wisdom that both older and younger persons can share.

Biblical wisdom to guide the encounter across the generations is captured in two passages. Philippians 2:34 suggests: "Do nothing from selfish ambition or conceit, but in humility regard others as better than yourselves. Let each of you look not to your own interests, but to the interests of others." This passage continues to describe the spirit of Jesus as being one of humility that applies to each generation in their interaction. The second passage is James 1:19b: "let everyone be quick to listen, slow to speak, slow to become angry." Communication is facilitated by active and empathetic listening that is a skill to develop over time, and with a commitment to remain in relationship for the long haul. Love, patience, and a willingness to speak and hear the truth are what sustain this relationship with youth. Adults are called to model effective communication in their relationships with youth and fostering their personal encounter with God.[9] Drawing upon Jesus' youthful encounter with the teachers in the Jerusalem Temple, I suggest that:

> Effective education occurs when people listen attentively and sensitively, raise questions based upon what they hear and discern, and share with integrity, as a gift to others, the wisdom they have gained. Such education assumes interpersonal interaction and willingness to dialogue.[10]

Adults need to allow space for the ministry of youth to find expression in their communal and corporate life. Freedom to fail allows youth

---

9. See my discussion of youth and God in Pazmiño, "Nature of God," 35–50, that includes a consideration of Jesus, Mary, and Joseph as youth.

10. Pazmiño, Latin *American Journey*, xii.

the opportunity for learning that allows for the operation of God's grace, just as Jesus' parents did on their trip to Jerusalem.

ADULTS

With much emphasis upon the growth and development of both children and youth the transitions and changes of adults across their life span may be ignored in practice if not in psychological research. Jesus' own adult journey from Galilee to Jerusalem in his public ministry portrays a variety of transitions and challenges. Becoming his own person in relation to his mother's expectations, along with patterns of interdependence, are considered in chapter seven in an in-depth look at the wedding at Cana. His relationships with Nicodemus and the Samaritan woman Photini, discussed in chapter nine, capture dimensions of outsider and insider dynamics in interpersonal life that impact one's self understanding. Jesus models for all humanity the realistic struggles of human existence and the choices persons make in their journey through adulthood. In Jesus' case his adult life on earth ended at about thirty-three years, but a host of other biblical personages live through young, middle, and older adulthood. Their lives can serve as witnesses for contemporary settings and persons as Hebrews 12:1–2 suggests:

> Therefore since we are surrounded by so great a cloud of witnesses, let us lay aside every weight and the sin that clings closely, and let us run with perseverance the race that is set before us, looking to Jesus the pioneer and perfecter of our faith, who for the sake of the joy that was set before him endured the cross, disregarding its shame, and has taken his seat at the right hand of the throne of God.

Jesus' example of addressing suffering and shame with joy and purpose provides encouragement for the challenges of adult life and the possibilities of faith, hope, and love that transcend the immediate human dilemma of transition and loss. For teaching adults, the example of Jesus noted in Hebrews 12 suggests attentiveness to suffering, transition, and loss along with faith in God's grace and provision. Hebrews 12:12 makes explicit God's help and healing for the adult journey in practical terms: "Therefore lift up your dropping hands and strengthen your weak knees, and make straight paths for your feet, so that what is lame may not be put out of joint, but be healed."

Adults, as they age beyond young adulthood, have the responsibility for being the mentors and guarantors of the growth and development of the rising generations. This assures a continuing legacy for the faith and wider community. Advocacy for "the common good" described in 1 Corinthians 12:7 is essential in the United States where a destructive individualism and presentism have eclipsed commitments to the wider community and society. Tax cuts for the wealthy of today do not consider the legacy for future generations in terms of the national debt in the United States. Shortsighted greed must be confronted among adults who have power and authority in corporate decisions in political, economic, social, and religious spheres. The example of Jesus was the laying down of his life for his friends: "No one has greater love than this, to lay down one's life for one's friends" (John 15:13). This verse adorns a statue in the Cathedral of Saint John the Divine that is a tribute to the firefighters of New York City who have died in their service to the metropolitan community. I have always remembered that statue I first saw in 1978, and especially in the light of September 11, 2001. Being a native New Yorker, the statue and the prayer of Father Mychal Judge, a Fire Department chaplain who died at the World Trade Center, are etched on my memory. Father Mychal's prayer I first heard when a former doctoral student of mine, Brian Jordan, who was Mychal's Franciscan colleague on national television, shared it. This prayer captures the openness to service for the common good that each adult can embrace as a continuing legacy of Christian discipleship:

> Lord, take me where You want me to go;
> Let me meet who You want me to meet;
> Tell me what You want me to say, and
> Keep me out of Your way.

Father Mychal Judge carried a copy of this prayer with him and prayed it each day to focus his life in the spirit of Jesus. Teaching adults can potentially foster a life of discipleship that is willing to be sent and witness to Jesus' spirit who is alive and well in the third millennium. Jesus' spirit invites adults to see all persons as potential friends or neighbors rather than "the other" in today's divided world.

FAMILIES

Given the fragmentation in the wider society and community, families as mediating institutions between larger systems or structures and persons have experienced greater pressures.[11] Survival takes on an all-consuming character in the light of various new demands. The increased limitations on one's ability as a parent to respond daily pose a dilemma. Various forces contend for the value formation of children and youth in ways inconsistent with closely held parental perspectives. The reality that both a village and congregation are needed by parents to raise children requires the formation of partnerships and alliances that are not a part of the inherited fabric of communal life. Even with these challenges, the insight of Lawrence Cremin regarding the educational history of the United States is still applicable: "The education of the home is often decisive and educative styles first learned in the family hold much of the key to the patterns by which individuals engage in, move through, and combine educational experiences over a lifetime."[12] Families do have to contend with the increasing presence and seductive impact of the media, but parents and caretakers still make choices and need the support of local churches to be wise in their choices. Like with individual persons, and as modeled by Jesus at Cana, families need to maintain a healthy independence and interdependence in their relationships with the wider community and society. This poses a daily challenge with the variety of influences upon the lives of children and youth. The potential positive influences of families in our lives are celebrated while recognizing the negative influences on the development of children, youth, and adults in some cases. With this recognition, the insights of James Loder who affirmed the transformative workings of God across the life span, is important. Loder noted that "development is not destiny."[13] God's grace can bring healing to the ravages of dysfunctional families through adoption into God's family.

Being a recently blessed grandfather, I have particular concerns for the world that will be a legacy for my grandchild. Families who have the support of their extended family relationships in close proximity are less the norm with increased mobility on a global scale. With this reality the support of local church communities for families takes on additional importance. A family focus in the local church should not come at the

---

11. The pressures identified in Keniston, *All Our Children*, persist twenty-five years after the initial research. The pressures included doubts about proper child rearing practices, changes in family structures, increased economic and social limitations, and a new role to meet social needs unsupported by extended family and communal networks.

12. Cremin, *Traditions of American Education*, 122.

13. Loder, *Logic of the Spirit*, 142.

expense of inclusion for single adults that could hypothetically exclude the person of Jesus who was also a single adult himself in his earthly journey.

COMMUNITIES

With the increased urbanization of the human race, the need to intentionally support and sustain local communities takes on additional importance. Communities serve as mediating or buffering agencies in society for how societal forces impact individuals along with families and congregations. Persons of faith have a public role to play in seeking the welfare of the city, suburb, village, or town where they reside. This is the model for believers who found themselves in exile within communities not exclusively godly in character:

> Thus says the Lord of hosts, the God of Israel, to all the exiles whom I have sent into exile from Jerusalem to Babylon: Build houses and live in them; plant gardens and eat what they produce. Take wives and have sons and daughters; take wives for your sons, and give your daughters in marriage; multiply there, and do not decrease. But seek the welfare of the city where I have sent you into exile, and pray to the Lord on its behalf, for I its welfare you will find your welfare. (Jer 29:4–7)

For Christians who affirm the lordship of Jesus Christ, faith values and issues have social, political, economic, and cultural expressions. This is the nature of created social life. The character of communal life is passed on to the rising generations through the regular face-to-face interchange across the generations. Teaching in its formal, nonformal, and informal expressions forms the lives of persons across the life span. How we live together communicates a wealth of lessons imbibed by children from their birth and even prior to conception. Attention to the quality and ethos of communal life is the responsibility of adult members and leaders of a community. Too often leaders, even those identified as persons of faith, have not modeled the quality of life that best represents Christian values noted in part one of this work: truth, love, faith, hope, and joy. While recognizing the effects of sin, the openness to God's grace experienced in forgiveness and reconciliation is essential in the life of local communities. The impacts of racism, sexism, classism, and oppression in various forms breaks the bonds of the human community and the one human race God created to bring glory and enjoyment to the world.

CONCLUSION

A comprehensive agenda is set for teaching the Christian faith with children, youth, adults, families, and communities in being responsive to persons in the postmodern twenty-first century. The very spirit of Jesus Christ is a partner with Christians called to teach in this world with all of its promise and problems. That partnership enables Christians to teach in the power of Jesus that is explored in part three.

PART THREE

Teaching in the Power of Jesus

I N A WORLD PREOCCUPIED with the use and abuse of power, teaching in the power of Jesus requires definition. While writing this introduction I am sitting in sight of a summer thunderstorm with attendant heavy downpours and frequent lightning strikes across the landscape. A flood watch has also been issued for the surrounding county with rising rivers and creeks in this Midwest town of Crawfordsville, Indiana. With the lightning I am aware that the electrical power for the computer I am using may be intermittent. As a result I am frequently saving my text. A tornado watch has also been issued with the national severe weather warning system, and I am aware where to go for safety in this newly constructed building. The potential negative impact of natural power surrounds me even when indoors. The sheer powers of the natural world are reminders of God's power in all of life, even as the earth groans with continental drift and the shifting plates of the earth's crust.

My thoughts are being recorded in a recently completed state of the art conference center at Wabash College. I am conscious of the power of financial resources to realize a dream and plan for such a facility, in part used to empower effective teaching practice among educators gathered from across the country. Having arrived to this center by air travel, I was conscious of the power of a jet engine to lift the contents of a plane sitting close to its operation at the rear of the airplane. While en route I prayed for the participants and leadership of the conference, including myself, being conscious of my reliance upon a higher power, namely God to be present in all the events scheduled for the upcoming six days. The positive impacts of financial, technological, and spiritual power sources surround me in this educational context and en route to it. I am not always conscious of these power dynamics in my normal daily activities. Power of various kinds surrounds us each day with both potential positive and negative applications. What then does the power of Jesus have to do with teaching today amid the powers of human existence on this planet? How is power understood in Jesus' ministry as love and service, as compared with force or coercion in human affairs?

Chapter nine considers the power of Jesus manifested in his encounter with two persons as recounted in the gospel of John. One person, Nicodemus, represents an insider in religious circles of Jesus' time and one, the Samaritan woman, an outsider from the perspective of his first-century Jewish religious community. Jesus effectively and powerfully communicated with each of these persons, crossing borders in the process. Both the insider and outsider learned from their encounters with Jesus. Jesus' power as a teacher brought transformation into their lives.

Chapter ten proposes how the power of teaching relates to transformation that is a theme many educators have explored both within and outside of religious educational circles and discussions. Teaching can serve to inform, form, and potentially transform persons and their relationships over time, fulfilling the call of Jesus in the third millennium, just as was the case in the first millennium. The methods and means may vary, but the result in new life can be as awesome as a thunderstorm and as subtle as a drop of rain upon a parched or soaked land.

9

The Power of Jesus in Teaching Insiders and Outsiders

THE REACH OF JESUS' teaching extends to all persons to include those identified as insiders and outsiders in any religious community. In the gospel of John this is made most apparent for me in Jesus' encounters with Nicodemus and the Samaritan woman, recorded respectively in chapters 3 and 4.[1] Nicodemus and the Samaritan woman encountered Jesus in everyday life. The contrasts between the two accounts are worthy of study by Christian teachers.

Nicodemus came at the end of the day, perhaps under the cover of the night to avoid recognition. He was the consummate insider in the Jewish community being a member of the Sanhedrin. He was privileged and empowered, and may have overcome an initial prejudice about Jesus in seeking him out at all. Whereas Nicodemus encountered Jesus in the cool of the night, the Samaritan woman came in the heat of the midday. Her appearance at this time suggests outsider status even among others in her Samaritan community, itself a community of outsiders among Jews, including Jesus and his followers. The Samaritan woman overcame her initial shock of contact with a Jewish male to engage a transformative conversation on spiritual matters.

Jesus provided tutorials for both Nicodemus and the Samaritan woman, even as their status as insider and outsider provide striking contrasts. Jesus' example is suggestive for how contemporary teaching relates to those who are both dominant and marginal in various teaching contexts. With these first-century persons, the power of Jesus' teaching

1. It is noteworthy that Lois E. LeBar, who looked to the scriptures for buried educational treasure, is also drawn to both the Samaritan woman and Nicodemus in John's gospel. She explores Jesus' teaching within the chapter "The Teacher Come From God," in her *Education that is Christian*, 63–76.

95

to bring personal and communal transformation is extraordinary and instructive for Christian teachers in the twenty-first century.

Jesus in his earthly ministry was conscious of the dynamics of all communities that establish insiders and outsiders. John 1:11 notes that "He came to what was his own, and his own people did not receive him." Jesus was crucified outside the gates of Jerusalem (Heb 13:13–16) bearing the shame of the cross and exclusion.[2] As exemplified in Jesus' ministry, God makes outsiders insiders and insiders outsiders with reversals unanticipated. Jesus invites all to become outsiders in being adopted as insiders, as children of God.

JESUS AND THE INSIDER: NICODEMUS

Recorded in the gospel of John, chapter 3, is an encounter extensively commented upon in noting Jesus' call to conversion of one noted for his religious credentials. Nicodemus was a religious leader and a member of the Jewish Sanhedrin, a select group of seventy members who governed religious life in the occupied Roman province of Judea. He was the consummate insider in Jewish community life who came to Jesus at night seeking a private encounter. It is noteworthy that Nicodemus identified Jesus as a "teacher who has come from God." I have often wondered why at night. I have thought that Nicodemus was perhaps avoiding the gaze of others in seeking contact with Jesus who was viewed as an outsider from the perspective of the Sanhedrin. Raymond Brown noted that the night (v. 2) symbolizes evil, untruth, and ignorance, but from his encounter with Jesus and his teaching, Nicodemus goes out into light (vv. 19–21).[3] Here we have the religious leader and insider seeking to learn from the noted outsider about spiritual matters. This pattern is often repeated in religious communities, as those in power need to gain a perspective they often fail to see being at the center of religious life. Those on the margins, the outsiders, can only afford this perspective. In his encounter with Jesus, Nicodemus poses a number of crucial questions: "How can anyone be born after having grown old? (John 3:4). Can one enter a second time into the mother's womb and be born? (John 3:4). How can these things be?"

2. See Costas, *Christ Outside the Gate*. Costas invites Christians to a mission with the outsiders of our time in the light of Jesus' example of identifying with the suffering of those outside.

3. Brown, *Gospel According to John (I–XII)*, 130.

(John 3:9). The posing of such questions assumes that Nicodemus is open to inquiry and learning, though his full comprehension is questionable. The text suggests that Nicodemus received extensive teaching from Jesus on the matters under discussion. Jesus' teaching can be viewed in trinitarian form with emphases upon the role of the Spirit (vv. 3–8), the role of the Son of Man (vv. 11–15), and the role of God the Father (vv. 16–21).[4]

Though Nicodemus himself was identified as a "teacher of Israel" (v. 10), his full grasp of Jesus' teaching and his hoped-for transformation is not noted in this particular passage of chapter 3. This suggests to me, that in the case of Nicodemus and other religious insiders, the process of transformation and conversion often extends over time rather than a more immediate response, as was the case for the Samaritan woman recorded in the following chapter of John's gospel. Why might this be the case? Those on the inside are afforded power and privilege that are not readily surrendered in responding to Jesus' call for transformation and discipleship. The stakes are greater and the resistance stronger in moving from what is viewed as the center to the margins where Jesus resides. This does not mean that there is no hope for Nicodemus and other well-positioned insiders to understand the teaching and experience the transformation Jesus promised. Later passages in John's gospel expand upon the transformation Nicodemus experienced over time and his willingness, though well positioned, to disclose publicly his faith in Jesus. Though Jesus was an outsider from the Sanhedrin's religious perspective, Nicodemus did see him as the "teacher who has come from God" (v. 2), with much to teach all generations of potential followers.

Nicodemus is noted in two other passages of John's gospel that are suggestive for proposing a process of faith transformation, in his case in contrast with the radical and sudden changes evident with the Samaritan woman in chapter 4. First, in John 7:45–52, the gospel writer in the context of a report to the Jewish leaders of Jesus' public teaching and disclosure at the Festival of the Booths in Jerusalem, records the following:

> Then the temple police went back to the chief priests and Pharisees, who asked them, "Why did you not arrest him?" The police answered, "Never has anyone spoken like this!" Then the Pharisees replied, "Surely you have been deceived too, have you? Has any one of the authorities or of the Pharisees believed in Him? But

4. Ibid., 136. Also see my discussion of the place of the Trinity in Christian teaching in Pazmiño, *God Our Teacher*, 15–36.

this crowd, which does not know the law—they are accursed." Nicodemus, who had gone to Jesus before, and who was one of them asked, "Our law does not judge people before first giving them a hearing to find out what they are doing, does it?" They replied, "Surely you are not also from Galilee, are you? Search and you will see that no prophet is to arise from Galilee."

Nicodemus was one of the Pharisees, and in this public and highly charged review of the temple police's report, defended Jesus' right to a fair hearing. The religious authorities fail to acknowledge the teaching authority of Jesus that the temple police clearly recognize. Jesus' association with Galilee qualifies him as an outsider among the Jewish leadership, and Nicodemus' appeal to legal procedures associated him with a similar outside status in public perception. The irony of Nicodemus' defense of Jesus suggests that he, as a religious authority and Pharisee knowledgeable in the law, believed in Jesus or at least enough to defend his rights with his insider colleagues.

Second, in John 19:38–42, after the tragic death of Jesus on the cross, Nicodemus accompanied Joseph of Arimathea to bury him in Joseph's tomb:

> After these things, Joseph of Arimathea, who was a disciple of Jesus, though a secret one because of his fear of the Jews, asked Pilate to let him take away the body of Jesus. Pilate gave him permission; so he came and removed his body. Nicodemus, who had at first come to Jesus by night, also came, bringing a mixture of myrrh and aloes, weighing about a hundred pounds. They took the body of Jesus and wrapped it with spices in linen cloths, according to the burial custom of the Jews. Now there was a garden in the place, where he was crucified, and in the garden there was a new tomb in it in which no one had ever been laid. And so, because it was the Jewish day of Preparation, and the tomb was nearby, they laid Jesus there.

Here is a striking public display of faith on the part of Joseph who was a secret disciple of Jesus now going public. By implication, Nicodemus also made public his faith through bringing the burial spices and participating with Joseph in the burial of Jesus. An irony of this account is that Jesus the outsider is afforded an insider's burial at the hands of a wealthy leader, Joseph, and a religious leader, Nicodemus. This was a costly venture for Nicodemus the insider to embrace a faith in the Galilean outsider, prophet, and teacher Jesus. Nicodemus' journey to public discipleship was longer, but just as dramatic as that of the Samaritan woman in terms of potential witness and impact.

INSIDER CHALLENGES IN DISCIPLESHIP

Three challenges stand out in relation to Nicodemus' journey of faith affirmation as an insider within the Jewish religious community. First from John, chapter 3, we learn that insiders can be relatively uninformed and naïve about the full implications of Jesus' teaching and the possibilities of transformation. Being in a privileged and empowered position tends to support the status quo, particularly if any change involves a relinquishment of one's position and the experience of discontinuities with the current arrangements in a religious or broader community.

A second challenge emerges from John, chapter 7, where the vulnerability of insiders is noted. Insiders quickly become suspect as outsiders, given the precarious positions they hold. This is particularly the case when an insider advocates for those viewed as outsiders in public and explicit ways. By defending a fair hearing for Jesus the Galilean, Nicodemus was readily identified with Galilee and a vulnerable outsider status. The costs can be high in questioning communal norms and the assessments of "others" identified as outsiders. Jesus in his own earthly ministry associated with those on the margins of the Jewish community and was identified with them: "And as he sat at dinner many tax collectors and sinners came and were sitting with him and his disciples. When the Pharisees saw this, they said to his disciples, 'Why does your teacher eat with tax collectors and sinners?'" (Matt 9:10–11).

Third, we learn from John 19:39 that insiders may be called to take prophetic and vulnerable actions to address injustice and the suffering of others, now to be viewed as neighbors rather than others. Nicodemus after the crucifixion had an ally, Joseph of Arimathea, and they both took on expensive ventures in offering a rock-hewn tomb and one hundred pounds of spices for what appeared to be a defeated and dead leader. Here was a costly discipleship that embraced a public witness in difficult times. The allegiance of both Joseph and Nicodemus, identified as disciples of Jesus, overcame the fears in their explicit association with the crucified criminal placed on public display in his trial and crucifixion. No further mention is recorded in the scriptures of the devotion of Nicodemus in his discipleship, but the emergence of the followers of the Way (Acts 9:2) in Jerusalem provided the occasion for his explicit affiliation with the emerging Christian Church following Pentecost. The apostle Paul reflects upon the status of insiders in the life of the Christian community in 1 Corinthians 1:26–31:

> Consider your own call, brothers and sisters: not many of you were wise by human standards, not many were powerful, not many were of noble birth. But God chose what is foolish in the world to shame the wise; God chose what is weak in the world to shame the strong; God chose what is low and despised in the world, things that are not, to reduce to nothing things that are, so that no one might boast in the presence of God. He is the source of your life in Christ Jesus, who became for us wisdom from God, and righteousness and sanctification and redemption, in order that. As it is written, "Let the one who boasts, boast in the Lord."

One of my seminary professors pointed out that Paul noted that it is not *many* that are wise, powerful, or of noble birth, not suggesting that there were not *any* wise, powerful, or of noble birth. Nicodemus qualifies as one of those "any" if not "many" of insider standing among Jesus' followers. My professor's comments encouraged us as students to be diligent in our studies to gain wisdom. Therefore there is a place for the insiders like Nicodemus in Jesus' ministry and mission in the world. Their challenges like with the rich young ruler may be formidable, but not insurmountable, in being Jesus' disciples. "For God all things are possible" (Matt 19:26). Hope exists for insiders and outsiders alike in following Jesus who is their wisdom, righteousness, sanctification, and redemption for now and eternity.[5]

The gradual and generative process of Nicodemus' transformation indicates the sustaining power of Jesus' teaching over the years spanned by John's gospel account, from Nicodemus' nightly visit to Jesus' crucifixion and death. The sudden and dramatic process of the Samaritan woman's transformation in John, chapter 4, indicates the radical and total power of Jesus' teaching in her life. That total power is like the transformation a sudden rainfall can bring to a dessert landscape, issuing in new life bursting forth in a variety of colors and shapes. The Song of Moses captures the potential of such life-changing teaching: "May my teaching drop like rain, my speech condense like dew; like gentle rain on grass, like showers on

---

5. For a comprehensive work on discipleship, see Habermas, *Complete Disciple.*

new growth" (Deut 32:2). Rain can not only bring sudden and dramatic growth in a parched landscape, but also sustain growth over the long haul. Both short and long-term processes are signs of God's grace and mercy in creation and the new creation made possible in Jesus Christ.

JESUS AND THE OUTSIDER: THE SAMARITAN WOMAN

The contrasts between the Samaritan woman and Nicodemus are multiple. Their societal status and propriety alone could be graphed at opposing poles on any psychometric or sociometric scale. The social, religious, and cultural distance between Jesus and the Samaritan woman was great. Nevertheless, Jesus' encounter brought transformative teaching to bear upon her personal and social life in dramatic ways. Jesus crossed a variety of borders to relate to the woman he encountered at the well in the heat of the day. The distance between the Samaritan and Jew was greater than what existed between Jesus and Nicodemus, but the process of transformation in her case was dramatic and even radical by comparison with that for Nicodemus. What could account for some of these striking differences?

Being at the well at the heat of the day, the Samaritan woman had an outsider status even among Samaritan women in her town. This may well be related to the series of husbands she had had and her then-current domestic arrangement. The other women would likely come to the well at earlier and cooler times of the day. Having had five husbands and then living with one who was not her husband (John 4:18) was beyond the social norms of this first-century Samaritan community. This Samaritan woman's life would raise serious questions about her acceptability among Samaritan insiders. The disclosure in John 4:29 that Jesus had told her everything she had ever done resulted in everyone in the city going out to see him in person. The woman on the margin of acceptability and social decorum brought a transformative witness regarding the person and ministry of Jesus with her. John's text recorded in 4:39 the following: "Many Samaritans from the city believed in him because of the woman's testimony, 'He told me everything I have ever done.'" As a result of this encounter, Jesus stayed on for two days in their city. Whereas he often moved on from other Galilean and Judean settings, he found a hospitable setting for his teaching ministry with outsider Samaritans transformed by the witness of their own outsider, the woman Jesus met at the well. The Samaritan woman remained unnamed in the gospel account, whereas

Nicodemus is identified by name. The outsider is transformed and was used by God to bring transformation into the lives of many others through her witness. Other Samaritans put their faith in Jesus because they heard for themselves and were certain that Jesus was "truly the Savior of the world" (John 4:42). A religious and spiritual transformation impacted the lives of many Samaritans who embraced the teaching of Jesus the Jew. Jesus' ministry came through a woman who was an outsider among outsiders from the perspective of proper Jewish society of the first century. Church tradition names the Samaritan woman "Photini," which literally means "the enlightened one." She is also identified by Orthodox tradition as an apostle and evangelist to the Samaritans.

OUTSIDER CHALLENGES IN DISCIPLESHIP

Distinct from those challenges faced by insiders like Nicodemus, the Samaritan woman faced challenges in her faith journey upon encountering Jesus and his radical teaching related to her life situation. Given experiences of exclusion, the first challenge was one of credibility and recognition of her person. This is evident in the Samaritan woman's first question for Jesus in John 4:9: "How is it that you, a Jew, ask a drink of me, a woman of Samaria?" (Jews do not share things in common with Samaritans). Jesus recognized the Samaritan woman as a person with whom to have interaction and to share in common the need for water, both physical and spiritual waters. With the social, cultural, religious, and gender divide between the Samaritan woman and Jesus, the breach was not insurmountable.

The second challenge, once an interpersonal relationship was established, was the moral distance with the interest in the living water Jesus promised that would issue in eternal life. For this second challenge to be addressed, the Samaritan woman had to recognize her sinfulness manifested either in her personal choices or patterns of abusive relationships and choices that had others sin against her. Recognition of the pattern also assumed a willingness to find alternatives related to God's grace, forgiveness, and reconciliation made available in Jesus.

The third challenge for the outsider Samaritan woman was spiritual in nature, related to Jesus' teaching: "God is spirit, and those who worship him must worship in spirit and truth" (John 4:24). This third challenge was confronted in the recognition of Jesus as the Messiah for whom she and her people longed. Jesus would proclaim all things to her and the Samaritans who had ears, hearts, and minds responsive to God's visitation in the person of Jesus who drank with her at the well.

All who see themselves outside the Christian community and who thirst for the living water that issues in eternal life over the centuries and across cultures today, are not unlike the challenges the Samaritan woman and her people from the neighboring city faced. Jesus' transformative teaching has the power to address the challenges and cross the borders and boundaries that beset the human community that is composed of one human race from the creation. As much as cultural, ethnic, and national distinctives are to be celebrated reflecting the beauty and variety of creation, the common bonds across humanity are affirmed in the person and teaching of the second Adam, Jesus of Galilee. Jesus' teaching ministry and that of his witnesses extend beyond Jerusalem to include "all Judea, Samaria, and the ends of the earth" (Acts 1:8). The Samaritan woman was one of those witnesses whose testimony brought many Samaritans from her city to hear Jesus' teaching: "They said to the woman, 'It is no longer because of what you said that we believe, for we have heard for ourselves, and we know that this is truly the Savior of the world.'" The power of Jesus' teaching extended well beyond his personal interaction with the Samaritan woman to include many Samaritans from her city.

Jesus' interaction and teaching with the Samaritans was astonishing and instructive to his disciples. Jesus modeled for them the reach of his teaching to include those clearly identified as outsiders and beyond the pale of Jewish interest. He also modeled the nourishment he valued of doing the will of God who sent him on his teaching mission. The spiritual mission and nourishment was valued beyond the physical food he needed for sustenance (John 4:34). My colleague Valerie Dixon suggests that the nourishment Jesus valued was later embodied in the elements of the Lord's Supper that includes both bread and cup. The bread denotes the need for sustenance and the cup denotes joy. Both sustenance and joy are needed to extend life as God intends it to be lived among all people. Jesus did not discount the importance of sustenance related to both bread and water, but placed a higher value upon doing God's will that brings joy to human hearts and sustains the human community along with all of creation. Jesus attended to both bread and cup with a clear sense of priority in his teaching with the Samaritan woman and her city neighbors. The Samaritans welcomed Jesus as a neighbor and received his teaching that transformed their lives. One contemporary example of an effort to reach outsiders comes from the experiences of my brother-in-law Wayne who has been involved in a creative ministry called "Theology on Tap" in Wisconsin. This ministry shares a PBS program "The Question of God" narrated by Dr. Armand Nicholi that in nine conversations compares C. S. Lewis and Sigmund Freud's life views in actual bars followed by theological discussions of each segment. This ministry reaches outsiders like Jesus did at the Cana wedding with wine.

TRANSCENDING INSIDER AND OUTSIDER REALITIES IN JESUS

Jesus' teaching makes possible the transcending of insider/outsider dynamics that have plagued the human race from its inception. Being adopted into God's family by responding to Jesus' teaching and following him as a public disciple makes possible a new life-affiliation and commitment. The late missiologist and church leader Orlando E. Costas, in his work *Christ Outside the Gate*, cited the Hebrews passage that makes explicit Jesus' association with outsiders:[6]

> Therefore Jesus also suffered outside the city gate in order to sanctify the people by his own blood. Let us go to him outside the camp and bear the abuse he endured. For we have no lasting city, but we are looking for the city that is to come. Through him, then, let us continually offer a sacrifice of praise to God, that is, the fruit of lips that confess his name. Do not neglect to do good and to share what you have, for such sacrifices are pleasing to God. (Heb 13:13–16)

Nicodemus eventually was willing to go outside the gate to bury the body of Jesus along with Joseph. He was vulnerable in doing this good and willing to share one hundred pounds of costly spices. Likewise, the Samaritan woman shared what she had, the news of her encounter with Jesus. She was vulnerable in doing this good, given her standing. She took the further step of inviting fellow Samaritans to encounter Jesus themselves. Jesus' crucifixion and death outside the gate, that Nicodemus no doubt witnessed, broke down the barriers between the inside and outside of human communities.

The apostle Paul made explicit what Jesus' life, death, and reconciling ministry made possible for the human race in bringing together Gentile

6. Costas, *Christ Outside the Gate*.

and Jew and, by implication, other insiders and outsiders in the human community:

> But now in Christ Jesus you who once were far off have been brought near by the blood of Christ. For he is our peace; in his flesh he has broken down the dividing wall, that is, the hostility between us. He has abolished the law with its commandments and ordinances, that he might create in himself one new humanity in place of the two, thus making peace, and might reconcile both groups to God in one body through the cross, this putting to death that hostility through it. So he came and proclaimed peace to you who were far off and peace to those who were near; for through him both of us have access in one Spirit to the Father. So then you are no longer strangers and aliens, but you are citizens with the saints and also members of the household of God, built upon the foundation of the apostles and prophets, with Christ Jesus himself as the cornerstone. In him the whole structure is joined together and grows into a holy temple in the Lord; in whom you also are built together spiritually into a dwelling place for God. (Eph 2:13–22)

The first-century Christian church that may well have included both Nicodemus and the Samaritan woman, as described in the book of Acts, struggled with the realities of having Jew, Samaritan, and Gentile persons and communities to become one in their following Jesus. Over the centuries similar struggles have persisted in fulfilling the prayer of Jesus recorded in John's gospel that his followers might be one:

> I ask not only on behalf of these, but also on behalf of those who will believe in me through their word, that they may all be one. As you, Father, are in me and I am in you, may they also be in us, so that the world may believe that you have sent me. The glory that you have given me I have given them, so that they may be one, as we are one, I in them and you in me, that the world may know that you have sent me and have loved them even as you have loved me. Father, I desire that those also, whom you have given me, may be with me where I am, to see my glory, which you have given me because you loved me before the foundation of the world. (John 17:20–24)

Jesus' followers included Nicodemus, the Samaritans, and all who across the centuries, whether insiders or outsiders, have believed and followed him. All of these persons become one in Jesus Christ and witness to the world his transformative teaching and its power. The apostle Paul celebrates this reality in Galatians: "As many of you as were baptized into Christ have clothed yourselves with Christ. There is no longer Jew or Greek, there is no longer slave or free, there is no longer male and female; for all of you are one in Christ Jesus" (Gal 3:27–28). There is in Christ no longer insider and outsider for all are one.

IMPLICATIONS FOR TEACHING

Besides what is noted above, Lois Le Bar identified several basic principles for Christian teaching that were the same for both the Samaritan woman Photini and Nicodemus:

- Jesus started where persons were in the life journeys

- He responded to the questions they posed for him from their minds

- He aroused curiosity and questions through his interaction

- He directly stimulated others to ask leading questions

- Jesus met personal spiritual needs

- He related new insights to previous understandings that persons had[7]

To these I would add the purposeful dynamic of inviting transformation as Jesus himself trusted in the work of God's Spirit to work quite differently in both Photini's and Nicodemus' lives, in both outsiders and insiders. Chapter ten explores the power of teaching for transformation that Jesus exemplified in John's gospel.

---

7. LeBar, *Education that is Christian*, 75–76.

The Power of Teaching for Transformation

MEMORABLE MEALS

TEACHING IS DIRECTLY RELATED to education, which can be defined as a process of sharing content with persons in the context of their community and society. A metaphor for this process is the preparation of a feast placed upon a table welcoming all to participate. A few memorable meals shared with others over my sixty years of life come to mind, including my son's wedding rehearsal and reception meals. Content in teaching can include cognitive, affective, behavioral, and intentional dimensions with the hope of fostering learning on the part of participants, similar to meeting the needs of wedding guests. Learning itself requires the receptivity and participation of persons in the process, if discovery and transfer of the content is to be integrated into life. Without the ownership of the learning, participants can accumulate experiences, like meals, that do not result in any changes in their personal or corporate lives.

Teaching and learning can effectively conserve activities that become traditions or practices. These are often done without reflection upon the "what" and "why" of the content. Teaching of this kind is just as necessary for continuity in corporate and personal life as basic nutrition is essential to sustain life. The dimension of transformation requires additional dynamics that are considered in this chapter. Transformation represents the power of Jesus in the educational process and allows for discontinuity or change at crucial life-turning or transition points. Jesus came to offer new life and the experience of conversion itself brings transformation with a noted proviso identified by C. S. Lewis.

C. S. LEWIS ON GROWTH

C. S. Lewis, a lay theologian and author, noted that growth in life requires both continuity and change: "Mere change is not growth. Growth is the synthesis of change and continuity, and where there is no continuity there is no growth."[1] Change without continuity produces distortion and continuity without change produces stagnation in human affairs. Matthew 13:52 suggests such in describing Christian discipleship that draws both old and new treasures from the storehouse of the scriptures: "Therefore every scribe who has been trained for the kingdom of heaven is like the master of a household who brings out of his treasure what is new and what is old."[2] Both the old and the new are honored, and require a creative blend of perspectives in the ongoing life of any community. Walter Brueggemann describes this blending in terms of two elements of the Old Testament canon that affirms the continuity of the *ethos*, found in the law, and the discontinuity of the *pathos*, found in the prophets. The mediating third element between *ethos* and *pathos* is *logos*, found in the wisdom tradition that offers perspective in balancing the continuity and discontinuity in specific contexts and with particular persons, groups, and communities.[3] Teaching in the power of Jesus upholds wisdom, for in Jesus are hidden all the treasures of wisdom and knowledge (Col 2:2–3). Wisdom in the Christian tradition honors the place of both continuity and change in teaching to assure the growth of persons, communities, and societies in the ways God intends. These ways invite transformation.

TRANSFORMATION

I am proposing that the power of Christian teaching resides in information, formation, and transformation shared and explored with others in their learning together. Transformation is the particular focus of this chapter. Nevertheless, wisdom requires attention be given to the three dimensions of teaching—information, formation, and transformation—following the example of Jesus. Information is required to gain a basic understanding of Christian faith, and also of God, who initiates that faith. Formation is required to nurture the spiritual growth and development

1. Lewis, *Selected Literary Essays*, xxi, 330.
2. See Conde-Frazier, *Multicultural Models*, 267.
3. Brueggemann, *Creative Word*.

of persons in conformity with God's will and God's call upon their lives.[4] Transformation, particularly as evidenced in the lives of Nicodemus over time and the Samaritan woman in a shorter time span, call attention to Jesus' ministry. God's grace is operative and effective, in both the process of sharing information and fostering the formation of persons and communities. But similar to how the miracle at Cana (John 2:1–11) demonstrated a sped up process of the natural process of transforming the water in a grapevine into new wine, transformation can bring into fruition the impacts of information and formation in dramatic and noteworthy fashion.

Transformation in general can be defined as the process of going beyond existing or dominant forms to a new or emergent perspective and reality. The potential of transformation provides hope for persons and groups viewed as outsiders in the life of communities, for those on the margins.[5] This was the case for the Samaritan woman whom Jesus met at the well in John 4. In the face of the destroyers of life, transformation holds the promise of new life and possibility. Those destroyers can include injustice, war, poverty, racism, sexism, abuse, guilt, shame, and oppressions of various forms. Powers and principalities described in the Bible plague the human condition and consort with the matrix of personal and corporate sin, not unlike the matrix in the popular film series.[6] God's remedy for the persistent problem of personal and corporate sin is offered in the life, death, and resurrection of Jesus the Master Teacher. Such a radical claim is transformative of the acts of teaching and learning, a concept that deserves the attention of educators both inside and outside of the Christian tradition.

STEPS OF TRANSFORMATION

James Loder researched the process of transformation and suggested five steps that characterize its experience. The steps provide guideposts for teaching practice that seek to invite persons to be open to

---

4. For a recent comprehensive work on the ministry of formation see Yust and Anderson, *Taught By God*.

5. See my discussion of transformative Christian education in Pazmiño, *Latin American Journey*, 55–75.

6. See Pazmiño, *God Our Teacher*, for a discussion of sin related to teaching.

transformation.[7] From the Christian perspective transformation can be seen as a work of the spirit of Jesus upon the spirits, hearts, and lives of persons in the third millennium. From the perspective of Christian theology this can apply both to Christian education and general education of the public. It can also apply to education in other religious traditions through the operation of common grace and general revelation as an aspect of God's plenitude, which is the abundant fullness of God's grace.[8] Such a claim affirms the place of special grace and revelation that Christians celebrate in Jesus Christ. It also affirms the universality of the cosmic Christ and God's goodness manifest in a variety of forms.[9] Christian teaching can embrace the particularity of the gospel and its universalistic implications for teaching of the common good for all of creation. In theological terms, both the creative and redemptive covenants of God are affirmed for Christian teachers in the third millennium postmodern context. Postmodern developments invite a wider engagement of Christian theology with the public realities of God's creation and the interplay between Christians and non-Christians. This exploration is carried out in the search for truth that preoccupies education in general, and religious education in particular.[10] Loder's work on the process of transformation provides insights for Christian teachers.

LODER'S FIVE STEPS OF TRANSFORMATION

Loder identifies five steps for transformation, including conflict in context, interlude for scanning, insight felt with intuitive force, release and repatterning, and interpretation and verification. Each of these steps can be directly related to teaching as I have discussed in *Basics of Teaching for Christians*.[11] In summarizing that earlier discussion, I suggest that for the first step, conflict in context, a teacher can invite transformation by posing questions and problems to persons. As Abraham Heschel observed,

---

7. See Loder, *Logic of the Spirit*, and his earlier work, *Transforming Moment*, 3–4.

8. See Heim, *Depth of the Riches*, 123–296, for a discussion of the plenitude of God's grace.

9. See my discussion of religious pluralism in Pazmiño, *By What Authority?*, 119–46.

10. Pazmiño, *God Our Teacher*, 161–72.

11. Loder, *Transforming Moment*, 3–4. I discuss the relationship between each of these steps and teaching in Pazmiño, *Basics of Teaching*, 61–62.

"religion begins with a question and that theology begins with a problem."[12] Engaging persons requires their participation in the process of critical inquiry and searching for truth, that questions and/or problems can invite. This first step also requires that the teacher be sensitive to the present and wider context of persons and their perception of a connection to their settings and lives. Conflicts are not avoided in the first step, but are carefully confronted for what they can offer.

The second step, an interlude for scanning, fosters a safe and hospitable space for exploration that provides viable options for consideration. Scanning presupposes openness to new perspectives and possibilities not previously considered. It is also occasioned by the question or problem posed. New voices can be heard and responses initiated in the process of scanning. Scanning assumes receptivity and openness to transformation.

The third step, insight felt with intuitive force, is the breakthrough or enlightening that for the person of faith involves the work of God's grace in persons' lives. For Christians this step honors the person and work of the Holy Spirit who works in partnership with the spirits of the teacher and students in an educational setting. Wisdom is discerned or discovered and moves the heart, soul, and body, in addition to the mind, toward receiving the gracious gift of insight. Insight is a gift of the Holy Spirit. "Outsight," to coin a term, can complement insight that calls for seeing the wider world through God's eyes or from God's perspective.

The fourth step, release and repatterning, supports the integration of the new insight into the framework of a person's world and life views with a holistic appropriation of the truth. As the new treasure is brought forth from the storehouse of God's plentitude, the old treasure as well is seen in a new light and with deeper appreciation (Matt 13:52).

The fifth step, interpretation and verification, allows for the wider sharing and dissemination of the wisdom personally gained with one's various relationships and associations. The end of this process is new life, which in spiritual terms brings integration, wholeness, and holiness. The scriptures describe this state as *shalom*, a peace that God intends for all of creation and humanity.

Rather than a rigid programming, Loder's steps provide suggestive insights of the work of the Holy Spirit who delights in bringing surprise and wonder into the human experience. These steps do provide hints for

12. Kimelman, "Abraham Joshua Heschel," 17.

how the human teacher can be open to the person and work of the Holy Spirit in the ordinary rhythms of teaching and learning. The teacher must also be flexible to allow God's Spirit to draw upon the spirit of each person both within and outside the times set apart for instruction. The teacher also needs to honor the teaching and learning that is nurtured among participants where persons learn much from peers in their interactions and dialogue.

A VARIETY OF MEDIA

The availability of computer technology has enhanced the opportunities for persons to interact outside any formal or nonformal learning with face-to-face encounters. In some cases the level of intimacy through electronic communication exceeds that experienced within group gatherings, especially for those who are more reflective and introspective in their preferred learning style. My personal preference is for face-to-face teaching exchanges. However, the socialization of the media has developed other competencies and vulnerability that educators need to consider in fostering transformation through structured teaching and learning. One of my former students, who came to seminary after retiring from a successful career in elementary school teaching and extensive publishing, has a vital Internet ministry. She communicates with teachers across the country, supporting them with their professional and personal challenges. She has also used the traditional technology of writing a book to support the spiritual life of public school teachers in their professional and personal lives.[13] Bobbi Fisher was open to new avenues for ministry in her retirement, and God has used her joyfully as an agent of transformation in the lives of others as she has opened her heart to the work of the Holy Spirit.

My own personal ministry of mentoring other teachers has been expanded through computer networking with folk I have never met face-to-face. I trust that God's Spirit works through a variety of media to accomplish the formation of persons as disciples of Jesus Christ. At the local church level, the offerings of a curriculum publisher are augmented through the availability of curricular planners. Users of the curriculum receive online access to advice and supplemental resources that can enhance their teaching ministries. Given the impact of the media,

---

13. See Fisher, *Teacher Book.*

periodic evaluation of technologies is required as with all teaching efforts.[14] Teaching itself can be analyzed in terms of the three phases of preparation, instruction, and evaluation.[15] Exploring the contours of transformation in relation to each of these phases can provide some specifics for understanding the power of teaching for transformation. These specifics complement the need to honor the place of mystery in the three phases of teaching: preparation, instruction, and evaluation.

TRANSFORMATION IN PREPARATION

Teachers are to carefully consider content, people and the context of their encounters, and the events and relationships involved. Conscious reliance upon the person and work of the Holy Spirit is occasioned through the practice of prayer for all elements of teaching. The New Testament book of James provides a suggestion for teachers:

> If any of you is lacking in wisdom, ask God, who gives to all generously and ungrudgingly, and it will be given you. But ask in faith, never doubting, for the one who doubts is like the wave of the sea, driven and tossed by the wind; for the doubter, being double-minded, and unstable in every way, must not expect to receive anything from the Lord. (Jas 1:5–8)

Even after twenty-seven years of full-time teaching experience, dynamics and challenges surface in every teaching event that require awareness of and reliance upon God's wisdom and grace made available through the Holy Spirit. With all my careful plans I must allow for the Spirit to speak beyond my notes, through the dialogue fostered, and from insights shared by participants. On a number of occasions students cite the unplanned sharing as the most significant learning for them, and I attribute this to the Spirit's work. Our destructive doubts limit the receptivity to God's wisdom. Constructive doubts can occasion the posing of questions and the search for wisdom.[16] In James 1:5–8 destructive doubt is contrasted with faith.

---

14. For a discussion of evaluation see Pazmiño, *Basics of Teaching*, 75–99; and Pazmiño, *Principles and Practices*, 145–68.

15. These three phases of teaching are analyzed in Pazmiño, *Basics of Teaching*.

16. See the insightful discussion of three types of doubt by Habermas, "Doubt Is Not a Four-Letter Word," 403–4.

In addition to the general prayer for God's wisdom in the planning and preparation for teaching, specific prayer for each of the participants and for the teachers themselves contributes to the sensitivity to others and the types of relationships fostered in teaching. One comment shared in a recent oral evaluation session for a completed course was that a student sensed that participants were cared for and loved in their experience in and out of the classroom. I attribute this perception, and my sensitivity to students' needs, to regular times of prayer for them and their situations, and for their focus in the course content as related to their particular callings. In ministering with a variety of persons, I, as a teacher, need God's wisdom and the Spirit's empowerment to respond in edifying ways with students. Students often enter my required courses with resentments and mixed motivations regarding the value of studying Christian education. All students at the graduate level have been educated for many years and a number of persons have had very negative experiences in education courses at the undergraduate level. Some of my students have completed masters and doctoral study in general education, and seriously question the worth of Christian education courses that purport to address the theological, philosophical, and historical distinctives of a Christian perspective. I most delight in their transformations, reported at the end of their study, recognizing the crucial role prayer plays as they ask God to work in their lives. This is quite the opposite from the initial course session. God can move upon their hearts and minds to experience a difference more than just in word, but in the practice of teaching and learning that I hope they will encounter together.

The other practices that have facilitated my preparation include arriving fifteen minutes prior to class to welcome students, engage them, and sense what it is they may be bringing to class. My particular setting, with block scheduling, facilitates this early arrival. Leadership for opening devotions is shared with class participants, and arriving early gives me the opportunity to assist devotion leaders with set-up. In addition, the extra time allows me to share any prayer concerns from students who are unable to attend class. Preparation also includes my review of newspaper and news items that may preoccupy students, or events and stories that relate to the topics of a particular session. My predecessor at Andover Newton, Maria Harris, had the memorable practice of removing her shoes at the first course meeting and requesting that students do the same. This action suggests the holy opportunity that teaching, learning, and study can provide as a form of worship to God. Creating an ethos of holiness contributes to a sense of God's presence in teaching. The sacrament of teaching and learning is God's gift granted to persons. This gift calls for our corporate stewardship and commitment.

In relation to the preparation of content for teaching, I find the need to reappropriate material I may have presented at least twenty times before to gain a new perspective and passion. If I am not enthused about the material, I can imagine the impact upon the minds and hearts of students will be significantly reduced. My commitments to the truth and importance of the content are crucial because they become clear in how I share the material and the extent to which I am willing to dialogue about its significance for others. This can be related to the "so what" factor that is often raised in a concern for the pragmatic application and implications of the teaching content.

TRANSFORMATION IN INSTRUCTION

The place of transformation in instruction itself has been related in practice to my willingness to attempt new methods and to encourage the expression of creativity on the part of participants. My efforts to relate my teaching to the actual learning of participants and to assess that connection has also allowed for transformative elements to emerge. In working with one group of faculty gathered for their professional development, I heard of one metaphor for teaching that potentially can squelch transformation. One teacher saw his teaching as throwing spaghetti upon the wall with no regard for what may stick in terms of the learning retained by the students. This graphic image, though memorable, suggests no or little accountability for the actual learning fostered by instruction.

While I recognize that my instruction can in no way guarantee the hoped-for learning, or even transformation on the part of participants, as a teacher I have the responsibility to assess the learning gained and to vary my approach and method to maximize the potential learning. Even during instruction I recognize the need for partnership with the Holy Spirit to effect change and transformation in the lives of persons. This requires attentiveness to unanticipated opportunities for expansion and contraction of prepared sequences of content to address the revealed and real needs of participants. The complementary challenge is to stay on task and avoid an unending stream of distractions. This is a particular concern for persons who are teacher-directed in their learning style. One is also called in instruction to balance over time both low- and high-context learning factors.

High-context learning refers to a relatively greater sensitivity to the immediate context and the persons present. A high-context learning style is characterized by cooperative and collaborative learning, concrete value, real-life settings, relationships over tasks, seeing the big picture, and doing several things at once. By comparison, a low-context learning style is characterized by independent learning, abstract values, critical thinking, tasks emphasized over relationships, seeing details, and doing specific things in focus.[17] High-context learning is less the norm in the United States. It involves reliance, to a greater degree, on peers and the surrounding environment to help make sense of experiences, and is generally accompanied by a more holistic and visual approach to reality as opposed to solely an analytical and verbal orientation.[18] This balance with high- and low-context learning points up the need for variety in instruction that is the spice of teaching as well as life.

Instruction involves such a wide variety of factors that the beginning teacher can easily become overwhelmed with all that can be considered. In teaching about the art and craft of teaching, I recommend that an interest in transformation focus upon one skill, method, or practice at a time. The self-reflective teacher needs a critical space to assess how any attempted improvement or change is perceived and received by participants. This is necessary because the performer or practitioner in the case of teaching initially perceives any change as awkward. Any new skill or approach, if it is to be transformative both for the teaching and learning experiences, requires the passage of time allowing for personal appropriation and reflection. Any change can also initially be perceived as a threat if persons do not understand the "what" and "why" of the change being experienced. Beyond the intellectual receptivity, persons respond at the level of their affections, attitudes, intentions, habits, and behaviors to any change that invites transformation. These levels can also be addressed in the instructional moves teachers engage in their practice. In my teaching, I work to develop anticipation for transformative experiences and allow

17. Breckenridge, "High/Low Context Groups," 334–35.

18. Wilson, "Pedagogical Expectations," 68–69. I explore some of these dynamics in relation to theological education with Hispanic persons in Pazmiño, "Theological Education with Hispanic Persons," 138–45.

for sufficient time for debriefing in fostering both the appropriation and transfer of the learning.

TRANSFORMATION IN EVALUATION

Evaluation with participants provides the opportunity to review the learning experience, invite further learning, and share what is more likely to be retained over time. Evaluation also provides the opportunity for persons to engage the fifth step of Loder's sequence for transformation, namely, interpretation and verification. Both written and oral evaluation can document and provide public confirmation of transformation that persons have experienced in their journey through a course or educational experience. When shared orally in the company of others, persons' individual learnings and transformative experiences can be confirmed and affirmed. Participants have often sensed that they are not alone in honoring what God has accomplished in their lives and how they hope to be responsible for their new learning. This sharing provides an occasion for the joy to be communal in nature. This joyful experience does not exclude the appropriate place for constructive criticism that can signal the possibility for future transformation in both the content and/or method of the teaching itself. The actual practice of evaluation, with sufficient time for both written and oral feedback, can model the place of transformation with the openness and vulnerability that teachers honor. Evaluation provides the occasion for teachers and participants to learn together in assessment, and to thank God for the workings of the Spirit through and even despite them.[19]

For the faithful practice of teaching, evaluation provides a necessary check on both the dangers of false pride and sloth in ministry. Teachers can celebrate the hoped-for transformation in lives when it occurs because they recognize and honor the work of God. The sufficiency for teaching ministry is of God in graciously using human persons like us to accomplish God's purposes (2 Cor 3:5). This eliminates a false pride that is preoccupied with being better than others. Genuine pride celebrates the privilege of service in response to God's call and using gifts from God.[20] Evaluation can also encourage future efforts with ones' commitment, time, and energy dedicated to the ministry of teaching. With all the possible

19. See my discussion of God despite us in Pazmiño, *God Our Teacher*, 37–57.
20. Pazmiño, *By What Authority?*, 74–75.

areas for improvement in the light of Jesus' exemplary teaching, sloth is not a real option for Christians.[21] Evaluation invites and anticipates future transformations in the practice of teaching.

CONCLUSION

The power of teaching for transformation, while explored in this chapter, must recognize the mystery of God's Spirit at work in the lives of persons who gather for teaching and learning together. This mystery relates theologically to the work of the Holy Trinity who replicates their shared life (*perichoresis*) in the human activities of teaching and learning.[22] Where the Spirit moves and directs teachers and learners, new life can be manifest that we name as transformation. No easy formulas or programs can direct the work of God's Spirit, but each teaching occasion can become a vehicle for God's gracious working in a plenitude of forms and techniques that honor the incarnation of Jesus the Christ as the Master Teacher. Jesus' ministry is replicated in the teaching ministry of those who follow his way and glorify God. This is transformation for teaching made possible today and in the years to come. The power of teaching for transformation is the privilege and responsibility of every Christian teacher.

21. See Pazmiño, *God Our Teacher*, 85–86, where I note Zuck's extensive list of principles and practices worthy of our emulation in teaching.

22. I explore the trinitarian connection in Pazmiño, *God Our Teacher*, 15–36.

Conclusion

IF THERE IS ONE lesson to be taken from this book it would be this: *Christians are called to boldly and lovingly teach in the name, spirit, and power of Jesus.* This is what makes our teaching Christian. After reading this work Christian teachers may have a renewed sense of our shared responsibility. In being a good steward of our calling and gifts, we cannot forget what the psalmist reminds us in Psalm 124:8: "Our help is in the name of the Lord who made heaven and earth." Claiming and embracing that name makes all the difference in our efforts by appropriating God's resources and answering in the affirmative Paul's question for us in Romans 8:32: "He who did not withhold his own Son, but gave him up all of for us, will he not with him also give us everything else?" God has provided all we need in Jesus Christ and the Holy Spirit in sharing the life of the Trinity in our teaching ministries.

The introduction to this work ended with my prayer. The prayer of the apostle Paul is a fitting close to this work where he links together the themes of Jesus' name, spirit, and power. This prayer is one that I offer for Christians who teach in a variety of settings today:

> For this reason I bow my knees before the Father, from whom every family in heaven and earth takes its name. I pray that, according to the riches of his glory, he may grant that you may be strengthened in your inner being with power through the Spirit, and that Christ may dwell in your hearts, through faith, as you are being rooted and grounded in love. I pray that you may have the power to comprehend, with all the saints, what is the breadth and length and height and depth, and to know the love of Christ that surpasses knowledge, so that you may be filled with all the fullness of God. Now to him who by the power at work within us is able to accomplish abundantly far more than all we can ask or imagine, to him be glory in the church and in Christ Jesus to all generations, forever and ever. Amen. (Eph 3:14–21)

Bibliography

Abba, Raymond. "Name." In *The Interpreter's Dictionary of the Bible*. Vol. 3. Edited by George A. Buttrick. Nashville: Abingdon, 1962.

Augustine of Hippo. *Augustine's Confessions*. Grand Rapids: Sovereign Grace, 1971.

———. "Prayer for the Indwelling of the Spirit." Patron Saints Index: Augustine of Hippo. Online: www.catholic-forum.com/saints/sainta02.htm.

Beyreuther. E., and G. Finkenrath. "Joy." In *The New International Dictionary of New Testament Theology*, 352–61. Edited by Colin Brown. Grand Rapids: Zondervan, 1971.

Boys, Mary C. *Educating in Faith: Maps and Visions*. San Francisco: Harper & Row, 1989.

———, ed. *Education for Citizenship and Discipleship*. New York: Pilgrim Press, 1989.

Breckenridge, James and Lillian. *What Color Is Your God?: Multicultural Education in the Church*. Wheaton: Victor Books, 1995.

Breckenridge, Lillian J. "High/Low Context Groups." In *Evangelical Dictionary of Christian Education*, 334–35. Edited by Michael J. Anthony. Grand Rapids: Baker Academic, 2001.

Brown, Raymond E. *The Gospel According to John*. Garden City, NY: Doubleday, 1966.

Brueggemann, Walter. *The Creative Word: Canon as a Model for Biblical Education*. Philadelphia: Fortress, 1982.

Buber, Martin. *I and Thou*. New York: Charles Scribner's Sons, 1970.

Burgess, Harold W. *Models of Religious Education: Theory and Practice in Historical and Contemporary Perspective*. Wheaton: Victor Books, 1996.

Carter, Stephen L. *Integrity*. New York: Basic Books, 1996.

Conde-Frazier, Elizabeth. "A Spiritual Journey toward Peaceful Living: From Hospitality to Shalom." In *Choosing Peace Through Daily Practices*, 158–85. Edited by Ellen Ott Marshall. Cleveland: Pilgrim Press, 2005.

———. ed. *Multicultural Models for Religious Education*. Atlanta: SPC/Third World Literature Publishing House, 2001.

Conde-Frazier, Elizabeth, S. Steve Kang, and Gary A. Parrett. *A Many Colored Kingdom: Multicultural Dynamics for Spiritual Formation*. Grand Rapids: Baker Academic, 2004.

Costas, Orlando E. *Christ Outside the Gate: Mission Beyond Christendom*. Maryknoll, NY: Orbis, 1993.

Cremin, Lawrence A. *Traditions of American Education*. New York: Basic Books, 1977.

Cully, Iris V. *Education for Spiritual Growth*. San Francisco: Harper & Row, 1984.

Dean, Kenda Creasy, and Ron Foster. *The Godbearing Life: The Art of Soul Tending for Youth Ministry*. Nashville: Upper Room Books, 1998.

Díaz, Miguel H. *On Being Human: U.S. Hispanic and Rahnerian Perspectives*. Maryknoll, NY: Orbis, 2001.

Bibliography

Downs, Perry G. *Teaching for Spiritual Growth: An Introduction to Christian Education.* Grand Rapids: Zondervan, 1994.

Dunn, James D. G. "The First and Second Letters to Timothy and the Letter to Titus." In *The New Interpreter's Bible: Volume XI, 2 Corinthians, Galatians, Ephesians, Philippians, Colossians, 1 & 2 Thessalonians, 1 & 2 Timothy, Titus, Philemon,* 773–880. Nashville: Abingdon, 2000.

Dykstra, Craig. *Growing in the Faith: Education and Christian Practices.* Louisville: Geneva Press, 1999.

Fackre, Dorothy and Gabriel. *Christian Basics: A Primer for Pilgrims.* Grand Rapids: Eerdmans, 1991.

Fackre, Gabriel. *The Christian Story: A Narrative Interpretation of Basic Christian Doctrine,* Rev. ed. Grand Rapids: Eerdmans, 1984.

Fisher, Bobbi. *The Teacher Book: Finding Personal and Professional Balance.* Portsmouth, NH: Heinemann, 2000.

Freire, Paulo. *Pedagogy of the Oppressed.* Translated by Myra Bergman Ramos. New York: Seabury, 1970.

García, Sixto. "United States Hispanic and Mainstream Trinitarian Theologies." In *Frontiers of Hispanic Theology in the United States,* 88–103. Edited by Allan F. Deck. Maryknoll, NY: Orbis, 1992.

González, Justo L. *Acts: The Gospel of the Spirit.* Maryknoll, NY: Orbis, 2001.

_____. *Mañana: Christian Theology from a Hispanic Perspective.* Nashville: Abingdon, 1990.

Green, Thomas F. *The Activities of Teaching.* New York: McGraw-Hill, 1971.

Groome, Thomas H. *Sharing Faith: A Comprehensive Approach to Religious Education and Pastoral Ministry.* San Francisco: Harper Collins, 1991.

Gross, Victor. *Educating to Reverence: The Legacy of Abraham Heschel.* Bristol, IN: Wyndham Hall, 1989.

Habermas, Ronald T. *The Complete Disciple: A Model for Cultivating God's Image in Us.* Colorado Springs: NexGen, 2003.

_____. "Doubt Is Not a Four-Letter Word." *Religious Education* 84 (Summer 1989) 403–4.

Harvey, D. "Joy." In *The Interpreter's Dictionary of the Bible.* Vol. 2, 1000–1001. Edited by George A. Buttrick. Nashville: Abingdon, 1962.

Heim, S. Mark. *The Depth of the Riches: A Trinitarian Theology of Religious Ends.* Grand Rapids: Eerdmans, 2000.

Herzog, William R. II. *Prophet and Teacher: An Introduction to the Historical Jesus.* Louisville: Westminster John Knox, 2005.

Heschel, Abraham J. *Between God and Man: An Interpretation of Judaism from the Writings of Abraham Heschel,* Edited by Fritz Rothschild. New York: Free Press, 1959.

Hess, Carol Lakey. *Caretakers of our Common House: Women's Development in Communities of Faith.* Nashville: Abingdon, 1997.

Isasi-Díaz, Ada María. *Mujerista Theology: A Theology for the Twenty-First Century.* Maryknoll, NY: Orbis, 1996.

Issler, Klaus. "The Spiritual Formation of Jesus: The Significance of the Holy Spirit in Jesus' Life." *Christian Education Journal* 4 (Fall 2000) 5–24.

Jones, Jeffrey D. *Traveling Together: A Guide for Disciple-Forming Congregations.* Herndon, VA: Alban Institute, 2006.

Bibliography

Jones, Kirk B. *Rest in the Storm: Self-Care Strategies for Clergy and Other Caregivers.* Valley Forge: Judson, 2001.

Kang, S. Steve. "Truth-Embodying Households." In *Growing Healthy Asian American Churches,* 39–57. Edited by Peter Cha, S. Steve Kang, and Helen Lee. Downers Grove, IL: InterVarsity Press, 2006.

Keniston, Kenneth. *All Our Children: The American Family Under Pressure.* New York: Harcourt Brace Jovanovich, 1977.

Kimelman, Reuven. "Abraham Joshua Heschel: Our Generation's Teacher in Honor of the Tenth Yahrzeit." *Religion and Intellectual Life* 2 (Winter 1985) 8–18.

LeBar, Lois E. *Education that is Christian.* Wheaton: Victor Books, 1989.

Lee, James M. *The Sacrament of Teaching, Volume 1, Getting Ready to Enact the Sacrament.* Birmingham, AL: Religious Education Press, 1999.

Lewis, C. S. *Five Best Books in One Volume: Miracles.* New York: Christianity Today, Iversen Associates, 1969.

_____. *Selected Literary Essays by C. S. Lewis.* Edited by Walter Hooper. London: Cambridge University Press, 1969.

_____. *Surprised By Joy: The Shape of My Early Life.* New York: Harcourt Brace Jovanovich, 1955.

Loder, James E. *The Logic of the Spirit: Human Development in Theological Perspective.* San Francisco: Jossey-Bass, 1998.

_____. *The Transforming Moment: Understanding Convictional Experiences.* 2nd ed. Colorado Springs: Helmers & Howard, 1989.

Lowell, James Russell as cited in David J. Bosch, *Transforming Mission: Paradigm Shifts in Theology of Mission.* Maryknoll, NY: Orbis, 1991.

McBride, Alfred. *A Retreat with Pope John XXIII: Opening the Windows to Wisdom.* Cincinnati: St. Anthony Press, 1996.

McKeachie, Wilbert J. *Teaching Tips: Strategies, Research, and Theory for College and University Teachers.* 9th ed. Lexington, MA: Heath, 1994.

McPherson, Alan M. "Sheer Joy." In *These Days: Daily Devotions for Living by Faith,* Vol. 33, No. 2, June 27, 2002. Louisville: Presbyterian Publishing Corp., 2002.

Mercer, Joyce Ann. *Welcoming Children: A Practical Theology of Childhood.* St. Louis: Chalice, 2005.

Moore, Mary Elizabeth Molino. "Sacramental Teaching: Mediating the Holy." In *Forging a Better Religious Education in the Third Millennium,* 29–50. Edited by James M. Lee. Birmingham, AL: Religious Education Press, 2000.

_____. *Teaching from the Heart: Theology and Educational Method.* Harrisburg, PA: Trinity Press International, 1998.

Moran, Gabriel. *Religious Education Development.* Minneapolis: Winston Press, 1983.

Murphy, Debra Dean. *Teaching that Transforms: Worship as the Heart of Christian Education.* Grand Rapids: Brazos, 2004.

Newell, Edward J. *"Education Has Nothing to Do with Theology": James Michael Lee's Social Science Religious Instruction.* Eugene, OR: Pickwick Publications, 2006.

Nouwen, Henri J. M. *In the Name of Jesus: Reflections on Christian Leadership.* New York: Crossroad, 1989.

Osmer, Richard R. *Teaching For Faith: A Guide for Teachers of Adult Classes.* Louisville: Westminster/John Knox, 1992.

_____. *The Teaching Ministry of Congregations.* Louisville: Westminster John Knox, 2005.

Bibliography

Palmer, Parker J. "Evoking the Spirit in Public Education." *Educational Leadership* 56 (December 1998–January 1999) 6–11.

_____. *To Know As We Are Known: Education as a Spiritual Journey.* San Francisco: Harper, 1993.

Pazmiño, Robert W. *Basics of Teaching for Christians: Preparation, Instruction and Evaluation.* Eugene, OR: Wipf and Stock, 2002.

_____. *By What Authority Do We Teach? Sources for Empowering Christian Educators.* Eugene, Ore.: Wipf and Stock, 2002.

_____. *God Our Teacher: Theological Basics in Christian Education.* Grand Rapids: Baker Academic, 2001.

_____. *Latin American Journey: Insights for Christian Education in North America.* Cleveland: United Church Press, 1994.

_____. *Principles and Practices of Christian Education: An Evangelical Perspective.* Eugene, OR: Wipf and Stock, 2002.

_____. "The Nature of God from an Adolescent Perspective." *The Journal of Youth Ministry* 1 (Spring 2003) 35–50.

_____. "Teachings of Paul." In *Evangelical Dictionary of Christian Education*, 686–88. Edited by Michael J. Anthony. Grand Rapids: Baker Academic, 2001.

_____. "Theological Education with Hispanic Persons: Teaching Distinctiveness." *Teaching Theology and Religion* 6 (July 2003) 138–45.

Pineda, Ana María. "Hospitality." In *Practicing Our Faith*, 34. Edited by Dorothy C. Bass. San Francisco: Jossey-Bass, 1997.

Scott, John R. W. "Am I supposed to love myself of hate myself? The cross points a way between self-love and self-denial." *Christianity Today* (April 20, 1984), 27–28.

Smith, Abraham. "'The First Letter to the Thessalonians: Introduction, Commentary, and Reflections." In *The New Interpreter's Bible: Volume XI, 2 Corinthians, Galatians, Ephesians, Philippians, Colossians, 1 & 2 Thessalonians, 1 & 2 Timothy, Titus, Philemon*, 671–737. Nashville: Abingdon, 2000.

Solivan, Samuel. *The Spirit, Pathos and Liberation: Toward an Hispanic Pentecostal Theology.* Sheffield, England: Sheffield Academic Press, 1998.

West, Cornel. *Race Matters.* Boston: Beacon, 1993.

Wilkerson, Barbara, ed. *Multicultural Religious Education.* Birmingham, AL: Religious Education Press, 1997.

Wilson, Norman G. "Pedagogical Expectations of Hispanic Americans: Insights for Leadership Training." *Christian Education Journal* 1, new series (Spring 1997) 65–81.

Yust, Karen Marie, and E. Byron Anderson. *Taught By God: Teaching and Spiritual Formation.* St. Louis: Chalice, 2006.

Zuck, Roy B. *Spiritual Power in Your Teaching*, Rev. Ed. Chicago: Moody, 1972.

_____. *Teaching as Paul Taught.* Grand Rapids: Baker, 1998.

Index

Abba, Raymond, 18–20
access, 36
action(s), 11, 19, 25, 28, 41–43, 46, 99
acts, of teaching, 41–42
Acts, Book of, ix
admission, 7
adoption, 82
adults, 87–88
advocacy, 49–50
amazement, 24
anawim, 36, 48–49
anger, 47
anticipation, 50
attention, 50
Augustine, 31, 36, 47, 50
authority, 18–20, 24–25

Basics of Teaching for Christians
    (Pazmiño), 66, 110
belief, 72
Bible, xi, 43, 56, 121
Boys, Mary C., 46
Brown, Raymond E., 70–78, 96
Brueggemann, Walter, 108
Buber, Martin, 13
Burgess, Harold W., 46

call, 2
    of disciples, 75
Cana, 11–12, 69
    wedding of, 11, 69–79, 87
care, 19, 33–34
Carter, Stephen L., 27–28
celebration, 19, 60–61
challenge, 33
change, 108
children, 42, 84–85

Christology, 1
church, 76
    Christian, 8
citizenship, 45
commandment(s), 31–32
    new, 31
    two great, 22, 51–52
commission, 18, 35, 77
commitment, 44, 76
common good, 39, 88
community(ies), 21, 78, 90–91
compassion, 8–9
Conde-Frazier, Elizabeth, 37
confession, 7
continuity, 108
conversion, 48–49, 96–97
Costas, Orlando E., 104
courage, 19, 47
Cremin, Lawrence A., 89
cross, 9, 37, 52
crossing borders, 103
crucifixion, 1, 8–12, 15, 37, 59, 104
Cully, Iris V., 65

devotion, 44
dialogue, 4, 23, 35, 45–46, 51
discipleship, 45, 76–77, 99–101,
    102–04
discipline, 43
Dixon, Valerie, 103
doubt(s), 51–52, 113
Downs, Perry G., 65
Dunn, James, 81–82
Dykstra, Craig, 40, 42

east, 78

Index

education, 33
  definition of, 33
educational equity, 38–39
ethos (*ethos*), 11, 108
Eucharist, 72, 77
evaluation, 28–29, 117–18
event, 14–15
Ezra, 44, 61

Fackre, Gabriel, 24
faith, 2, 19, 40–46
families, 88–90
fiesta, 60–61
Fisher, Bobbi, 112
freedom, 4, 38, 48, 66, 85–86
Freire, Paulo, 25

Galilean principle, 14
Gamaliel, 57
glory, 70–71, 73–75
God Our Teacher (Pazmiño), 81
González, Justo L., ix, 60
good shepherd, 9–10
Gorman, Julie A., 23
grace, 2, 26, 73–74, 109–10
grandparenting, xii, 53, 89
Green, Thomas F., 41
Groome, Thomas H., 46
growth, 108

Habakkuk, 55, 62
Harris, Maria, 114
Heschel, Abraham J., 80, 110–11
Hess, Carol Lakey, 45
Hispanic community, 60–61
Holy Spirit, 33, 60, 71–72, 81, 113, 115
  See also Spirit
hope, 2, 7, 19, 33, 47–54
humility, 6–8, 38, 43, 86

incarnation, 1, 2, 15
identity, 1, 2, 8, 22
insider, 14, 99–101, 104–06

insight, 110–11
instruction, 115–17
integrity, 19, 27–28
Isasi-Díaz, Ada María, 49 n.6
Issler, Klaus, 82

Jesus, ix, 3, 7, 22, 31, 34, 73–75
  as exemplar, 5, 51, 82–83
John, ix, 58
John, Gospel of, ix, 12–13
John XXIII, Pope, 29
Jones, Kirk B., 35
Joseph of Arimathea, 98, 99
joy, 2, 19, 55–63, 74, 87
Judge, Father Mychal, 88
justice, 37–39

Kang, S. Steve, 15
kin-dom, 49

Lawson, Kevin E., 79
learning, 23–25, 40, 42, 107
  high-context, 116
  low-context, 116
LeBar, Lois E., 106
Lee, James Michael, 77
Lewis, C. S., 55, 74, 104, 107–08
liberation, 83
life, 13, 22, 78
listening, 86
Lines, Timothy A., 46
Loder, James E., 89, 109–12
logos, 108
Lord's Supper, 72, 77
love, 2, 19, 31–39
  cruciform, 37–38
  of teaching, 35–36
Lowell, James Russell, 30

Mary, 70–71, 76–77
Mary Magdalene, 78
meals, 107
media, 112–13
memory, 50

Index

mentor(ing), 38, 85, 112
mission, 40–41, 76
Mission of Nombre de Diós, 17
model, 1–2, 38, 45, 82
Moore, Mary Elizabeth Molino, 62

name, 17
    bearing, 53
    of Jesus, 17–63
Nehemiah, 61
Nicodemus, 12, 14, 87, 94–99,
    104–05
Nombre de Dios mission, 17
north, 78
Nouwen, Henri J. M., x, 3, 31

opposition, 59
oppression, 39
orthopathos, 61
Osmer, Richard R., 46
outsider, 14, 101–06
outsight, 111

Palmer, Parker J., 23, 65
paradox(es), 4–6, 56
particularity, 21, 110
Passion of the Christ, 9
pastoral task, 25
pathos, 108
Paul, 4, 57, 100
Pazmiño, Oliver A., xi, 48, 63
peace, 26, 37, 49, 105
perichoresis, 118
persons, 34–35, 78
Peter, ix, 34, 58
Photini, 87, 102
    Also see Samaritan woman
Pilate, 10
plenipotentiary manner or role, 2, 18
plenitude, 110
popular prophet, 3
postmodernism, 21, 110
power, 12–13, 19, 93–94, 100
prayer, xii, 4, 33–34, 36, 88, 114, 119
    Jesus', 4

preparation, 113–15
pride, 6, 44, 117
process, 13–15, 100
prophet(s), 3
prophetic task, 25

question(s), 14, 51–52, 97, 110

reconciliation, 26
relationship(s), 21, 87
Resurrection, 1, 12–14, 15–16

sacrament, 77
sacramental acts, 11
Samaritan woman, 12, 14, 94–95,
    101–02, 105, 109
    Also see Photini
scanning, 111
scripture, 24
service, 8–10, 44–45
shalom, 26, 49
show trial, 9
sin, 24–26, 45, 109
Smith, Abraham, 81
Solivan, Samuel, 61
south, 78
speak the truth in love, 19, 25, 66
Spirit, 73, 80–91
    God's, 5
    Holy, 33, 60, 71–72, 113
    of Jesus (Christ), x, 8, 71
    See also Holy Spirit
spiritual discernment, 23, 26, 80, 82
spiritual gifts, 23, 33
spirituality, 65
steadfastness, 28
suffering, 8–9, 56, 59–60, 87

table, 36–37, 49–50, 66, 75–76
table fellowship, 11–12, 50
teaching, 62, 106, 113
    activities of, 41–42
    phases of, 11, 32, 47, 82, 108, 113
theology, 1–16
    practical, 1

Timothy, 81
transformation, 25–27, 49, 97, 100,
    108–18
    definition of, 109
    five steps of, 109–12
trinitarian dysfunction, 24–25
Trinity, 25
truth, 2, 10, 15, 21–30
Tyrannus, school of, 52

universality, 21, 110

virtues, Christian, x, 2–4, 8

wedding of Cana, 11, 69–79, 87
Wesleyan roots, 24
west, 78
West, Cornel, 48
wine, 72, 74, 77–78
wisdom, 21, 29–30, 75–76, 86
witness, x, 3, 28, 101–02
woman, 102
    virtuous, 29
wonder, xi, 42, 56, 61, 65–66, 74–75
Wright, Dana R., xi

youth, 48, 80–81, 85–87

Zuck, Roy B., 65